W9-DJE-236

COPING WITH

A

Drug-Abusing

Parent

Lawrence Clayton, Ph.D.

THE ROSEN PUBLISHING GROUP, INC. NEW YORK

8-4-95

Published in 1991 by The Rosen Publishing Group, Inc.
29 East 21st Street, New York, NY 10010

Copyright 1991 by Lawrence Clayton, Ph.D.

First Edition

Library of Congress Cataloging-in-Publication Data
Clayton. L. (Lawrence)
    Coping with a drug abusing parent/Lawrence Clayton.—1st ed.
        p.   cm.
    Includes bibliographical references (p.   ) and index.
    Summary: Describes drug addiction, its symptoms and
manifestations: the effect of an addict on his or her family: how to
handle the pressures of living with an addict: and how to get help.
    ISBN 0-8239-1300-7
    1. Children of narcotic addicts—United States—Juvenile
literature.   2. Children—United States—Drug use—Juvenile
literature.   3. Narcotic addicts—United States—Family
relationships—Juvenile literature.   4. Co-dependence
(Psychology)—United States—Juvenile literature.   [1. Drug
abuse.]   I. title.
HV5824.C45C53   1991
362.29'13—dc20   90-24855
                                                            CIP
                                                            AC

Manufactured in the United States of America

To My Mother,
Nathalie Craig

ABOUT THE AUTHOR ◇

L awrence Clayton grew up in a small town in central Nevada. He became acquainted with the dynamics of life in a home with an alcoholic stepfather. His stepbrother was an addict and eventually committed suicide. His uncle, who was alcoholic, was also a suicide victim. Clayton joined the United States Army at the age of seventeen. He served three years in Germany and two years in Vietnam.

Dr. Clayton holds a Bachelor's degree from Texas Wesleyan College (summa cum laude), a Master's degree from Texas Christian University, and a Doctorate from Texas Woman's University.

Since 1971 he has specialized in treating children, youth, and families as an ordained minister, clinical marriage and family therapist, and Certified Drug and Alcohol Counselor. He founded and directs the Clayton Center, in Oklahoma City. Much of his work is with children from homes in which drugs and alcohol have played a significant role.

He is an Approved Supervisor for the American Association for Marriage and Family Therapy and Vice-Chairman of the Certification Board for Drug and Alcohol Counselors. He is also a nationally recognized workshop leader.

Dr. Clayton is the author of *Assessment and Management of the Suicidal Adolescent, Coping with Depression,* and *Coping with Being Gifted.* He serves as an Associate

Editor for a journal entitled *Family Perspective*. He has been listed in *Who's Who Among Human Service Professionals* for the past eight years.

Dr. Clayton, a single parent, lives in Piedmont, Oklahoma, with his two children, Larry and Rebecca.

Contents

1   What Is Addiction?   1

2   Addictive Substances   26

3   The Addictive Cycle   37

4   Addiction as a Disease   46

5   The Addicted Personality   51

6   Coaddiction   62

7   What Should I Tell My Friends?   84

8   Family Roles   91

9   You and Your Brothers and Sisters   109

10   How Your Parents' Addiction Affects You   112

11   Blowing the Whistle   136

12   The Recovery Process   141

13   Getting Help   154

14   What You Can't Change   160

Bibliography   170

Index   171

CHAPTER 1

What Is Addiction

Melanie remembers watching Sam pull a marijuana cigarette out of his coat pocket and snicker as he showed it to his friend John. They were sitting across the aisle from her in the last row on the school bus. They glanced at her and didn't seem to mind that she was watching as they lit it and passed it back and forth between them.

Phil came home early from his Boy Scout meeting to find his older brother Rob standing at their father's bar with a whiskey bottle in one hand and the teapot in the other. Rob started yelling at him for borrowing his headphones. That really surprised Phil because Rob had never seemed to mind before. He decided not to ask Rob why he was pouring tea into the whiskey bottle.

Marsha has been selling drugs to her friends at school for two years now. An adult friend named Reggie meets her in the parking lot on her lunch break. Marsha usually starts by giving a hit of speed or

LSD to friends at a party. Gradually, as they want more and more, she begins charging them.

Scott's Uncle Harry has been arrested often for driving drunk. Each time Uncle Harry calls Scott's mother to come and get him out. She always gets upset and cries a lot, but she does it. Scott's father becomes very angry when he discovers that his wife has paid Uncle Harry's fine and bailed him out again. Their fights are beginning to worry Scott.

We all know someone who uses drugs. It's just a sad fact of life these days—they're everywhere.

But what is the difference between someone who uses, or abuses, drugs and someone who is addicted to drugs?

And what if that someone is one of your parents?

To understand addiction it is important to look at some of the myths that keep people confused about addiction and what it is—and isn't.

Myth #1. All "real" alcoholics are skid-row bums whose families and employers have long ago given up on them.

Fact. Less than one-tenth of one percent of all addicts live on skid row. Most of the rest live with their families and go to work every day. To outsiders their lives appear quite normal.

Case Study: John is an electrical engineer. He has worked for the Alpha Company for fifteen years. He has been married to Phyllis for twenty-one years, and they have four children.

John started drinking beer when he was thirteen. At first he drank only on weekends, and then only a couple of cans of beer each day. By the time he was fifteen he was drinking a six-pack every Saturday and Sunday. When he was seventeen he was drinking a six-pack several times a week and as much as a case of beer on weekends.

Phyllis met John at a party in college. She was impressed with his ability to handle his liquor. That first night John drank at least ten cans of beer and a pint of whiskey and never appeared to be drunk. It wasn't long until they were going steady and partying every weekend.

After graduation John enrolled in engineering school and Phyllis got a job. Within three months Phyllis was pregnant. Her doctor told her that the parties would have to stop. When she told all this to John, he seemed elated about the pregnancy but somewhat upset about the parties. Still, he promised that he would quit.

Within a week he came home very late and very drunk. Once again he promised to stop. He didn't, but Phyllis was too happy with the prospect of her first baby to be very concerned. Soon John had graduated from engineering school and gotten a very promising job, and their future looked bright.

Ten years later they had four children and John was chief engineer of the company and president of the administrative board at their church. He was also drinking a quart of whiskey every Friday, Saturday, and Sunday.

This family live in an affluent neighborhood and drive expensive cars. And all four of the children are beginning to show, to some degree, the scars of children of alcoholics.

John is an alcoholic; that is, he is addicted to alcohol. Addiction is defined as *the loss of ability to control one's use of a mood-altering substance or behavior.*

Myth #2. People *become* alcoholics or addicts.

Fact. People do not become alcoholics or addicts; they are born that way. People who eventually become addicted are born with a genetic "code" that means they are much more likely than the average person to become addicted.

In that way addiction is similar to diabetes. People who are diabetic are born with a specific gene that at a certain age will make that person diabetic.

In everyone's brain is a chemical called endorphin. Endorphin has been called "Mother Nature's morphine," a sort of built-in natural high. It gives us a sense of peace and well-being. Endorphin is released into the brain at various times—after exercise, when we see a beautiful painting, when our team wins, when a person of the opposite sex tells us we're cute.

When a person without the genetic predisposition toward addiction uses drugs or drinks, his or her body breaks down the alcohol or drug into substances that the body uses or expels.

But when a person with a genetic predisposition toward addiction uses drugs or drinks, his or her body turns a portion of the alcohol or drug into something called THIQ. THIQ is a suppressor chemical, and what it suppresses is endorphin.

The more an addict uses, the more THIQ is produced. While temporarily making him feel better, the drug is also causing a by-product that will, in the end, make him feel worse. He will keep on using because the drug does make him feel better until more THIQ is produced.

Eventually most alcoholics or addicts drink or use not to feel better or get high, but just to feel normal—the way most of us do every day.

And that is why an alcoholic or addict is *always* one drink or one dose short.

Although research has yet to validate it, this same process is probably at work in the bodies of all people who are addicted to behaviors, such as workaholics or churchaholics.

Case Study: The first time Bob smoked pot he was fourteen. He really liked the "rush" he got. He felt euphoric—"high" and very happy and pleased with life and himself in general. At first a couple of hits a day from a joint (marijuana cigarette) were enough.

Within a year he was smoking an entire joint each evening. By the time he entered college he was smoking several joints a day. When he was twenty-five, Bob was lacing (adding) THC (a stronger drug) into each joint. At forty, Bob was smoking crack (a very potent form of cocaine). This is a condition called *tolerance*. Tolerance is a sign that a user is addicted and that THIQ is being produced. Graphically, addiction looks like this:

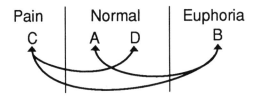

Before Bob started using, he was experiencing a normal mood (point A). When he used the first time, he got a euphoric "rush" (point B). Because of THIQ, he eventually was in pain whenever he wasn't using (point C). Finally, Bob was using just to feel normal (point D.) That was when Bob began to use more and stronger drugs.

Note: A word of warning is needed. Even though Bob's tolerance for drugs is increasing (that is, he is able to use more and more), he is moving closer and closer to the point at which the drugs will kill him. *There is only one difference between a drug and a poison, and that is the dose.* Any drug that will alter your mood will also kill you if used in large enough quantity.

Myth #3. Addicts lose control every time they use.

Fact. Addicts can control their use for limited periods of time. In fact, alcoholics and addicts often do without alcohol or drugs for a time to prove to themselves or others that they are not addicted. But they are in pain during this time, and they want to use or drink. The only valid "proof" is being able to stop using, not miss the drug, and not start again. In such a case the person is truly not addicted and will find other ways to enjoy life naturally.

Case Study: Oscar found himself using more and more speed. He started when he was driving a truck coast to coast. All the other drivers used it to help them stay awake. He justified the use of speed by telling himself that he was a safer driver. But now it seemed that he was always using, and he felt terrible when he wasn't.

Somewhere in a far corner of his mind was the nagging question, "Could I be addicted?" He had to know, so he decided to test himself. He would quit for a week. It was Monday, and he was determined.

By Tuesday he was "coming down," and he felt terrible. Wednesday he slept all day. Thursday and Friday were horrible; he felt as if his head were going to explode, and he was shaking all over.

Friday night he tried to watch television. By midnight he was in a bar drinking. "At least," he thought, "I'm not addicted to speed." Or was he? On Sunday he was using again. He had successfully lied to himself—until he suddenly found that his son, Oliver, eighteen and an honors student in his freshman year at the state university, was using speed to stay up all night and study.

Oscar's first reaction was fury, until his son convinced him that he, Oliver, was not addicted, either! The speed was just "useful"—it made him a better student, helped him keep his scholarship.

Oscar calmed down and accepted the explanation. Okay, both of them were all right. They weren't addicted. They just "used" now and then when it helped them.

But far below his conscious mind Oscar realized that something wasn't right, that he *and* his son were skating on thin ice. He refused to face the fact that he was addicted.

Remember, the worst lies addicts ever tell are the ones they tell themselves.

Myth #4. Once people are addicted to alcohol they drink until they pass out.

Fact. Some alcoholics *are* able to have one or two drinks and then quit on occasion. *But an alcoholic can never be sure that he or she will be able to have one or two drinks and then quit.*

Case Study: June had decided to cut down on her drinking. Lately she had been worried about some of the things she had done while she was drunk.

June worked in sales with several other people, and it had become a habit for them to stop off at a bar for a couple of drinks after work. Tuesday was no exception. But this time June had two margaritas and excused herself with, "I have a husband and two kids at home. See you later."

June's husband, Cecil, and their sons Tony and Kile were happy to see her come home the same time as other working mothers in the neighborhood. They were impressed when she told them that things were going to be different from now on. Impressed—but not quite believing. They'd heard that before. "From now on I'll be home every night by 6:30!" was greeted with an enthusiasm that was, shall we say, restrained. But, true to her word, June was home by 6:30 on Wednesday and again on Thursday. Even on Friday she managed to make it by 7 o'clock.

The weekend was uneventful, except that June's disposition steadily became worse. By Sunday afternoon she had screamed at everyone in her family, two neighbors, her mother—she had even kicked the dog!

On Monday evening the family went about their business at home very quietly, dreading what might happen. But June was home, and by 6:30 p.m.

On Tuesday she stopped off with her friends from work again, and this time she was swept out with the dust when the bar closed at two o'clock in the morning. On the way home she was arrested for driving under the influence. It was her third DUI and carried the very real possibility of a stiff prison sentence. Her children were terrified of that.

Myth #5. You're not an addict if you use only on weekends.

Fact. Addicts are of two basic types. One is the daily user. This type of addict may use all day long or only in the evenings. He may get very high or just stay tipsy for hours.

The other type is the binge addict. A binge addict uses mostly on weekends and holidays. But regardless of when he uses, he gets loaded almost every time.

Note: Daily addicts are easier to help than binge addicts. That is because a binge addict is accustomed to periods of abstinence followed by periods of drunkenness. The fact that a binge addict is straight adds nothing new to his pattern of use, whereas being sober is a new experience for the daily addict.

Case Study: Joe and Jeff are brothers. Both of them are addicts. Recently both of them entered treatment. Joe was the daily user type; Jeff was a binge addict. Right from the beginning the treatment staff noticed how different they were.

Joe went into severe withdrawal when he quit using. His body wasn't used to being without drugs. Jeff had no problem being without drugs, at least not for the first week. His body was used to being without drugs for extended periods of time.

After Joe got past his withdrawal symptoms, he was very cooperative and did well in the treatment program. Jeff was cooperative from the first day, but he craved drugs every weekend.

Both Joe and Jeff were discharged after thirty days of treatment. Joe never used again. Jeff managed to stay straight for two months. He has been in treatment five times since then, each time characterized by a period of abstinence followed by a relapse.

Myth #6. My parents' addiction is their problem. It won't affect my life after I grow up because I'll never use drugs.

Fact. When parents are addicted, everyone in the family is affected by it. The consequences of growing up in an addicted home can and usually do last a lifetime. The problems are so pervasive, so much a part of a child's personality and emotional pattern, that the effects can be passed down through several generations.

Even though you may never drink or use, your parents' addiction could cause problems that would make life difficult for your *grandchildren!*

Case Study: Marsha had always hated her father's using. Before it got so bad they were a happy family. Just like a sitcom on TV! Now, lately, Dad was hardly ever home, and when he was, she wished that he weren't. There wasn't any love in her family anymore. Her father was seriously depressed.

His angry outbursts were bad enough—then IT started.

The IT was sexual abuse, nights of terror when she lay rigid and listened as footsteps approached her room, days when she felt tormented by guilt, blame, and anger and tried to think what to do.

She believed that it was partly her fault and partly the result of her father's using. She promised herself that she would never marry someone who used and that she would protect her children from anything like what she and her sister had suffered.

When she was eighteen Marsha met Cal. He was just right for her: He was very religious and in fact was planning to become a minister. He never used and was strongly against drugs. They went together for two and a half years.

When Cal graduated from the seminary, they were married. Fourteen months later their first child was born. They named her Sarah.

Cal was dedicated to the Lord. He was determined. They were happy . . . almost.

The problem? Cal was upset with his church. It wasn't growing fast enough. The people weren't dedicated enough. He suspected that some of them used drugs or drank! And he preached angry, shouted sermons against this *sin!*

To Marsha, some of those sermons sounded a lot like her father's angry outbursts.

It wasn't long before the pastoral committee met and decided to fire Cal. They said there wasn't much love in his preaching—instead it contained much more judgment, condemnation, and blame.

Cal was unable to obtain another pastorate, and he went into a serious depression. Finally he got a job selling insurance. He seemed to work almost all the time. Marsha resented his work. She resented it as much as she had resented her father's using. When Cal was at home he was always either angry or depressed.

In fact, Cal seemed an awful lot like her father—but Cal didn't use drugs.

It wasn't until Sarah was fourteen that Marsha discovered the sexual abuse that her husband had been inflicting on her daughter. Marsha, horrified to the point of considering homicide or suicide or both, blamed herself, Cal's work, and the church that had fired him.

What never occurred to Marsha was that she had married a man with her father's personality, but who just didn't use drugs.

When Sarah was nineteen she met Ron. She felt comfortable around Ron. He seemed to have a lot of her father's personality except that he was less rigid and angry. In fact, he even smoked pot . . .

Note: This is just one of the many effects of addiction. Adults who grew up in addicted homes are affected and so are their children and their children's children. For that reason *it is essential for children of addicts to get professional help from a specialist in treating children of addicts.* If such help cannot be found while they are young, it is still crucial that they find it and work through their problems after they are adults.

Myth #7. Addiction can be cured.

Fact. An addict will always be an addict. An addict *can* be helped. He can get to the point of not using drugs (abstinence), but his body will always have an addictive potential. If he ever uses he will be addicted again. His body produces THIQ (see Myth #2) whenever he uses, and it always will. That will never change.

An addict or alcoholic who stops using can never use a mood-altering substance again. He can never learn to drink socially. He must remain drug-free for the rest of his life. Addiction can never be cured!

Many people who go through treatment think that they are cured. After a few months they deceive themselves into believing that they can drink socially. When they try, they soon discover that once again they are addicted.

Case Study: Brea had tried for years to beat alcohol and cocaine. She knew it was affecting her job, her relationship with her husband, Roy, the twins Bart and Brenda, and Conner. Brea had tried to quit by her own willpower over and over. She always failed.

But this time she had a plan! She had a month's sick leave built up at work, and she needed to have major surgery. She was scheduled to be in the hospital for a week. She talked her doctor into letting her stay two weeks. After that she was going to check herself into a chemical dependency program for two more weeks, telling her employer that she needed time to recuperate "at home."

After the surgery, the two weeks of treatment went well except that the staff at the treatment facility thought she needed an additional two weeks. But she was out of vacation time and needed to get back to work . . .

Brea stayed straight for three years. She often announced that she had no problem with alcohol or cocaine. She had "beaten it." She was cured.

On her twenty-fifth wedding anniversary she decided that she could drink a glass of wine to celebrate. She did. In fact, she drank two.

She didn't drink again for three days. Within a month she was using more cocaine than she had used before she entered treatment. Bart and Brenda both dropped out of college, Bart to go into the military and Brenda to marry a man she barely knew, "to get away from home, if you want the truth." Conner is thinking of running away and probably would if he didn't feel that his dad needed him.

Myth #8. A drug addict is improving if he switches to a less powerful drug or starts drinking alcohol instead.

Fact. When an addict uses a different mood-altering substance, he is still practicing his addiction. All mood-altering chemicals are addictive. If alcohol were a new drug on the market today, it would be available only by prescription. *Alcohol meets all the requirements established for narcotics.* (Narcotics are extremely dangerous drugs.)

Addicts who switch from a powerful drug like heroin to a less powerful drug like marijuana or alcohol will soon return to using the more powerful drug. They will also need more of it than they were using previously.

Case Study: Dan had been hooked on cocaine for ten years. He had done things to obtain cocaine that made him feel terrible about himself. His father owned the largest mobile-home lot in town, and Dan was his senior buyer.

Whenever someone traded a mobile home to another dealer, Dan was paged to bid on it.

Each time he bought a mobile home, Dan added $300 to the receipt. His father never questioned him. He trusted Dan; he saw no reason to quesion the son of whom he was so proud. Honesty had always been a great value in their family. Each time Dan spent the money on cocaine.

Finally Dan could stand it no more. He told his father about the cheating and that he was addicted. It was the first time Dan had ever seen his father cry. It was horrible!

But his father said he would help. He paid for Dan's treatment for addiction. On discharge from the hospital, Dan was referred to an outpatient counseling center. He met weekly with a therapist and seven other addicts. Talking to others made him anxious and nervous. He started smoking pot before meetings "to calm myself down. At least it isn't something as dangerous as heroin."

Buying mobile homes now also made Dan anxious. He wondered how many of the dealers knew about his addiction and his stealing from his father. Soon he was smoking pot or stopping off for a drink before going to bid on a trade.

One day he was driving past his drug dealer's house and decided to say hello. He was loaded by the time he left. The dealer had given him cocaine on credit. The next day Dan added $300 to the receipt he gave his father.

Danny Jr. knew about his father's "problem" and had been on the outs with him for several years because of it. Although Danny Jr.—known as D.J.—wanted to be close to his father, he found it very difficult, especially after he learned that Dan had cheated his grandfather, whom he adored.

That night Dan came home to find his wife upset and worried; $20 had disappeared from her purse. Although

D.J. was only 15, he was big for his age, and a few days earlier she had heard him on the telephone talking about a place where kids could buy beer "and if you look old enough they never bother to check your ID."

Myth #9. If I use drugs a few times nothing bad will happen.

Fact. That depends. If you have inherited a genetic tendency to produce THIQ, your first use will start the process described in Myth #2. Thus your first use may be exactly what sets the addictive process in motion. In addition, some drugs such as crack cocaine set the addictive process in motion much faster than others. With crack it is possible to become addicted in a single afternoon, or even with the very first use.

Other drugs have a high "overdose potential"; that is, it is easy to kill yourself the first time you use the drug. In fact, every time you use cocaine it is possible to make a mistake that could be fatal. That is largely because of the effect it has on your heart and central nervous system. You could have a heart attack—yes, even at your age!—a stroke, or go into a drug-induced coma.

It is important to understand how drugs are distributed in this country.

Drugs are passed from one supplier to another many times before they reach the users. Each supplier makes money by "cutting" the drug (adding ingredients to it).

Drugs have been cut with everything imaginable, including formaldehyde (which morticians use to embalm bodies), arsenic (a poison), even rat poison. You can never tell what is in a drug you buy on the street.

Occasionally drugs go directly from the supplier to the user without being cut. That can be even more dangerous. In 1985 a shipment of 97 percent pure cocaine was seized on the turnpike between Tulsa and Oklahoma City. It was so strong that anyone who used it could have died almost instantly.

Case Study: Jack had never used cocaine, but he had heard that it gave one of the best "highs" possible. He knew that his wife, Kathy, had smoked cocaine and that she loved it. Nothing bad seemed to happen to her because of smoking cocaine.

Jack had been a football player in high school and college. Not yet forty, he still worked out and was in perfect physical condition. He kept in touch with guys he had played football with in college. Some of them were in the NFL now, and he knew some of them used. And nothing bad had happened to them. "So, why not?" he reasoned.

The last thing Jack remembered was the horrible crushing pain in his chest. He was dead on arrival at Memorial Hospital. He had suffered a massive heart attack.

Jackie, thirteen, and Richard, ten, were left without a father and with a mother whose drug use was rapidly passing the "experimental" stage. Jackie thinks she can see what their future is going to be like, and it scares her half to death.

Myth #10. My dad can't be addicted. He only drinks beer.

Fact. There is approximately the same amount of alcohol in an eight-ounce can of beer, a glass of wine, a mixed drink, and a shot of whiskey. Some alcoholics drink only beer; others may drink wine, beer, or whiskey depending on what is available.

Case Study: Jacob loved beer. He knew all about beer. He knew how it was made, how it was shipped, and at what temperature it should be served.

He never drank "hard liquor." After all, "Only alcoholics drink hard liquor." He was just "a hard-working, hard-playing, good ol'boy from Georgia." He'd been drinking beer all his life.

Jacob never stayed late at the bars; after all, he had a wife and family to look after. He drank a beer every night as soon as he got home. At least, that's the way it was for the first eight years. Then things began to change. Jacob was drinking more and more until he was putting away six to twelve cans of beer every evening and from a case to a case and a half of beer on Saturday and again on Sunday.

His habits began to change. He stayed longer at the bars, and when he was home he watched television and drank beer late into the night.

Jacob also seemed angry most of the time when he wasn't drinking. He had become rigid, controlling, and forgetful. Things he forgot he blamed on his wife and sons. Sometimes he couldn't even remember how he had spent an evening. In short, Jacob was addicted to alcohol. Beer just happened to be his drug of choice.

Myth #11. People who are addicted simply lack willpower. They are weak or morally and spiritually sinful people.

Fact. Addiction has nothing to do with willpower. Addicts have lost control over a mood-altering substance or a mood-altering behavior. That does not happen because they are morally bad. It happens because they have inherited a genetic predisposition toward addiction.

Both medically and legally, alcoholism or addiction is classified as a disease. People who have it do not have a choice about it. They did not ask for it, any more than someone would ask for cancer or multiple sclerosis.

It may be that the only mistake they made was taking that first drink, and the overwhelming majority of people have had at least one drink in their lives. After that, the addiction process was set in motion and couldn't be stopped simply by willpower or "wanting to." It would take much more than that.

It is very important to remember that we should never hold an addict responsible for his addiction. After all, we don't hold a diabetic responsible for having diabetes. But we *can* hold an addict responsible for his recovery. Once an addict knows that he is an addict, he should be held responsible for doing something about it.

Help is available.

Case Study: Heather's mom always seemed to be such a loving person. The kids liked to come to her house. It was a fun place to be. But little by little Heather's mom began to change. She was angry a lot of the time and yelled at Heather and other kids for things she once would have thought funny. She became moody, unpredictable, harshly critical of almost everything.

Heather was thoroughly thrown by it all. She had no idea what was happening, or why. She began discouraging her friends from coming over, and she stayed away from home more and more herself. One day she realized how much her mother was drinking. She wondered if Mom were trying to drink her problems away—the fact that she was divorced, that money was tight, and things weren't going well on her job.

But those problems seemed to be getting better, not worse. Heather wondered what she could do. Trying to talk to her mother about it only drew anger. Heather felt helpless and scared.

In April, Aunt Mary come for a visit. She was Heather's favorite aunt, and for a little while things seemed happy at home again. Then one day Heather came home from school to find her mother and Aunt Mary in the middle of a terrible, screaming argument. Mom was yelling, "Oh, why don't you mind your own business! This has nothing to do with you!"

Aunt Mary screamed back, "It is my business and it has everything to do with me. You're the only sister I've got left. I love you, and you're letting alcohol destroy you and your whole family. Why, Heather told me she was ashamed of you and embarrassed to have friends come over anymore. Don't you see what's happening? Didn't you see enough of it with Dad? Just exactly the same thing is happening to you, and you're making Heather's life just like he made ours!"

Then Heather heard her mother crying and saying, softly, "OK, I'll go. You're right, I just wouldn't admit it, even to myself. But who'll take care of the kids?"

Aunt Mary said, "I will," as her niece walked in the door.

"What's going on?" Heather asked.

Mom was mopping tears, and Aunt Mary said, "Your mom is sick, and we're going to get help for her. Don't worry, everything is going to be all right. You wait here for the other kids to get home from school, and I'll be back in time to cook dinner for you all."

Miraculously, everything *was* all right. Mom was in the hospital a little over a month, and while she was gone Aunt Mary was such a pleasure for them all. Life was *fun* again.

When Mom came home she was different. She was the

way she used to be. She was seeing a therapist to help her cope with the divorce and with the problems that come with alcoholism. A financial counselor was helping her get money matters straight.

Soon Heather was inviting her friends over again. One day one of them said, "Heather, you've got the neatest mom in the whole world." Heather looked up just in time to see her mother begin to cry.

She jumped up and hugged her mom. "We're like a fairy tale. This story has a happy ending."

Myth #12. Sure, I'm addicted, but my habit will only hurt me. It's no one's business but mine. After all, it is *my* life."

Fact. Addiction is—unfortunately—everyone's business. It hurts everyone, even those who don't know the addicted person. Look at a few of the statistics. Drugs or alcohol are *directly* related to:

65% of all child-abuse cases
62% of all crimes
70% of all fatal falls
50% of all traffic deaths
67% of all suicide attempts
33% of all suicides
86% of all fire deaths
50% of all domestic battering cases
75% of all divorces
86% of all murders

Chemical dependency is estimated to cost $78.6 billion a year in the United States alone. It isn't just the addicted person's business. It is a national disgrace because although *we can successfully treat addiction, less than 1 percent of the chemically dependent ever receive treatment.*

Myth #13. I know Dad's an addict, but I'm too young to become addicted.

Fact. For drug addiction to become fully developed in a forty-year-old who just starts using could take up to twenty years. In a twelve-year-old it sometimes takes less than six months. That is because the twelve-year-old's body is still developing.

Case Study: Lucile was eleven and a half when she started using. By the time she was twelve she was using every day. Her grades had fallen, and she had became withdrawn and secretive. When her father put her in a hospital for what he thought was appendicitis, Lucile went into withdrawal, a sign of addiction of the most severe kind. In fact, Lucile almost died.

Case Study: Charles remembers his first drink very clearly. His father gave it to him when he was eight years old.

"I can still remember how good it tasted, how great it made me feel. I'll tell you the truth, I think I was an alcoholic from that very first drink."

By the time he was eleven, Charles says, "My life revolved around being sure I could get something to drink. I became good at getting Dad's liquor and watering down what was left so he wouldn't see how much was gone. Even when he guessed I'd been drinking, he thought it was more funny than serious. Sometimes I waited outside liquor stores, and when I saw people put booze in their cars and then leave again, I'd try to steal the liquor. I usually could, too."

By high school Charles, in his own words, "drank enough booze every day to embalm a dinosaur." He had

had his driver's license for three months when he ran a stop sign, drunk, and killed two people. He is now serving time in a juvenile correctional facility.

Myth #14. OK, so I'm addicted. If I simply stop using, everything will be just fine.

Fact. There is no guarantee that everything will be just fine. It depends on what, how much, and how long you've been using. There are primarily four problems with the idea that things will return to normal if an addict quits using.

1. If the person was addicted to an inhalant, he will have some degree of brain damage. All inhalants damage the brain; that's an inescapable fact. When a user quits, he generally will not get any better because damaged brain cells do not repair or replace themselves.

Alcohol also causes some brain cell damage that cannot be reversed, although to a lesser degree than inhalants.

2. If the person was addicted to psychedelics (drugs that cause hallucinations) such as PCP, LSD, mushrooms, or peyote, he may have flashbacks (reexperiences of a bad trip) for some time or permanently.

3. All persons who are addicted will have problems with *alcoholic personality syndrome*. They tend to be rigid, controlling, and angry, repressing all other feelings. They have problems with intimacy with another person. They tend to have low self-image, to be defensive and manipulative. Only professional help or self-help groups such as Alcoholics Anonymous or Narcotics Anonymous can do much to change this.

4. Alcohol and drug addiction also damage family relationships in such a way that only professional help can undo it. Children of addicted parents develop specific

characteristics that last a lifetime and are passed on to their children (see Chapter 14). In addition, the spouse of an addict almost always develops coaddiction (see Chapter 6).

Myth #15. Mom can't be addicted. She only takes medicine her doctor gives her.
Fact. Most chemical dependency counselors believe that about as many people are addicted to prescription drugs as are addicted to illegal drugs.

Case Study: Rhonda was seriously injured in a traffic accident. She spent weeks in the Intensive Care Unit and was still in a wheelchair when discharged from the hospital. It would take months of therapy and muscle-strengthening exercises before she would be able to walk again.

Rhonda was understandably angry at the way her life had been disrupted. During physical therapy, when confronted yet again with her limitations and how far she had to go to recovery, she would often explode into anger and then into tears. Her doctor gave her medication to help with the pain and sleeping pills to help her rest at night. She also had medication to relieve the anxiety and depression brought on by the long ordeal.

After eight months Rhonda was walking with only a slight limp, although she still tired very easily. However, she continued to take all the medications she had needed during the worst part of her recovery. When her doctor recommended slowly cutting back on the amount of medicine, she became angry and fired him.

Rhonda then began to "shop doctors," to go from doctor to doctor looking for several who would give her prescriptions for the drugs that her body had become accustomed to and now craved. At the present time she has sixteen doctors who prescribe medication for her. None of them know about any of the others. She takes three different types of painkiller, one anti-anxiety drug, one antidepressant, and three types of sleeping pills. She uses a different pharmacy for each doctor.

Rhonda needs more and more medication because she is developing a higher level of tolerance as time goes by. She occasionally frightens her husband and her children by mixing her medications and alcohol.

Rhonda is addicted and could die of an overdose at any time.

SUMMARY

Addiction is the loss of control over mood-altering substances.

Most addicts live in families and have jobs. People who know them fairly well might never guess they have a problem.

Addicts inherit a genetic potential for addiction. They are not bad people, nor do they lack willpower. They are able to not drink or use for short periods of time, but when they do use or drink they can never predict how much they will consume.

There are two basic types of addicts: the daily addict and the binge addict.

Addiction is a family disease; its effects can be seen for many generations.

Addiction can never be cured. An addict can never use a chemical without becoming more addicted. Severe problems can occur from just one use of an addicting chemical. Beer, wine, whiskey, amphetamines, narcotics, cocaine, psychedelics, inhalants, and barbiturates are all addictive.

Chemical dependency is a social problem because it affects everyone to some degree.

Anyone at any age can be addicted, but children and young people become addicted much faster than adults.

CHAPTER 2

Addictive

Substances

P eople have a natural curiosity about mood-altering drugs. Some of the questions most frequently asked are, "How many kinds of drugs are there?" "What are the proper and street names for these drugs?" "What are their medical uses?" "What do they look like?"

Those questions are answered in this chapter.

STIMULANTS

Amphetamines

Amphetamines are medically known by the names Benzedrine, Desoxyn, Dexedrine, Biphelamine, Dextroamphetamine, Methamphetamine, and Phenmetrazine.

The street names of these drugs include: dexies, uppers, pep pills, wake-ups, bennies, pushers, hearts, speed, meth, oranges, crystal, crank, bam, black beauties, glass of ice, white cross, black mollies, yellow jackets, bird-eggs, christmas trees, henis, black widows, and black birds.

The most common method of use is swallowing in pill or capsule form. The drugs can also be used in powder form and snorted, or in liquid form injected in a vein (called "mainlining").

Medically, amphetamines were once commonly used for weight reduction, although that is rare now. A central nervous system stimulant, they are used in treatment of diseases such as the scleroses and dystrophies or the condition called narcolepsy, or sleeping sickness.

The symptoms of amphetamine use are excessive activity, sweating, dryness of mouth, restlessness, increase in pulse and blood pressure, bad breath, mood swings, enlarged pupils, needle marks on arms or other areas where veins are easy to find, dizziness, wakefulness, talkativeness, irritability, irregular heartbeat, loss of touch with reality, and paranoia.

Use of speed over a long period of time, or a short period of very heavy use, can trigger outbursts of extreme, very dangerous, violence. An ambulance technician told of running a call for someone freaked out on amphetamines:

"He was inside this small house, and we sat in the ambulance and watched him literally tear the place apart. These people have the strength of King Kong. We saw him grab a section of window, and when he pulled half of the wall came out.

"When the cops got there and we went in after him it took eight of us to subdue him. In the brawl he got his arm broken, and that just barely got his attention."

In the book *Fatal Vision*, author Joe McGuinness writes about Jeff MacDonald, a doctor and a captain in the Green Berets. He speculates that MacDonald might have "flipped out" and gone on the rampage that ended in the murder of his pregnant wife and two small daughters after taking amphetamines to lose weight.

Other hazards of abuse of speed include brain damage, convulsions, hallucinations, paranoia, and death from overdose.

Amphetamines come in a wide variety of forms: pills, capsules, powder, liquid, or crystalline. Both crystal and the new designer drug ice come in crystalline form.

Cocaine

Cocaine is medically known by that name: cocaine.

The street names include coke, Bernie, toot, girl, C, white lady, snow, cecil, crack, nose candy, and blow. Crack, the designer form of cocaine, is an extremely fast-cycling stimulant to which persons can become addicted in one afternoon.

The most common method of use is by snorting (inhaling). It may also be swallowed, injected, or freebased (combined with another chemical and smoked).

Medically cocaine has a history of use as an anesthetic. It has no other known medical use.

The symptoms of use include excessive excitability, restlessness, nervousness, enlarged pupils, nausea, violent behavior, anxiety, paranoia, increased urination, loose stools, elevated blood pressure, feelings of well-being followed by depression, intense periods of euphoria, and increased pulse rate.

The hazards of abuse are damage to nasal passages, cardiovascular difficulties, and death from overdose. Recently, researchers have discovered that some persons lack a blood enzyme that breaks down cocaine. In these persons one experimental dose can prove fatal.

Like the amphetamines, cocaine use can set off rampages of extreme violence combined with almost superhuman strength.

Evidences of cocaine use include glass pipes, razor blades, white crystalline powder, syringes, needle marks on the arms or other places where veins are easily accessible.

DEPRESSANTS

Tranquilizers

Medically, tranquilizers are known as Phenobarbital, Secorbarbital, Nembutal, Amobarbital, Seconal, Amytal, Butizone, Noctec, Sopor, Liminal, Dramamine, Benadryl, Spairne, Lompazine, Mellaril, Thorazine, Phenergan, Nartec, Equanil, Miltown, Nolander, Doriden, Ativan, Xanax, Restoril, Halcion, Bonex, Valium, Dalmane, Serax, Quaalude, Centrax, Placidyl, Librium, Methaqualone, and Transiene.

The street names of these drugs are downers, goof balls, yellow jackets, barbs, red devils, blue devils, reds, tranks, blues, yellows, peanuts, numby dolls, Mickey Finns, jelly beans, sopos, goofers, peaches, ludes, 714s, muscle relaxants, and sleeping pills.

The most common methods of use are swallowing pills or capsules, or, in liquid form, injecting into a vein.

The medical usage is as a sedative in muscle spasms and nervousness and anxiety.

The symptoms of use are confusion, slurred speech, impaired judgment, disorientation, intoxicated behavior, depressed breathing and heartbeat, staggering gait, depressed blood pressure, loss of appetite, inappropriate feelings of well-being, drowsiness, and poor coordination.

The hazards of abuse are addiction with severe withdrawal symptoms, depressed cardiovascular functioning, and death from overdose.

Tranquilizers come in blue, red, yellow, and red/blue capsules, white or pale yellow powder, and liquid form. Evidences of usage include needle marks on skin, syringes, various containers with a powder or powder residue in them, or the finding of the tablets themselves.

Narcotics

Medically these drugs are known as Darvon, Percodan, Codeine, Heroin, Methadone, Morphine, Empirin, Tylenol with Codeine, and Darvocet-N.

The street names of these drugs are: horse, H, smack, boy, junk, dreamer, school boy, stuff, nord, sugar, tea, dolls, dolly, black tar, china white, joy powder, dope seat, harry, morph, and big M.

The most common methods of use are swallowing in pill form and injecting into the arm or other place where the veins are available. Some forms may be used rectally.

Medical usages include pain relief and, in the case of methadone, withdrawal from other narcotics.

The symptoms of use are euphoria, drowsiness, slurred speech, lethargy, needle marks, constipation, narrowed pupils, flushed skin (face, neck, and chest), respiratory depression, nausea, chills and sweating, cramps, watery eyes, tremors, cold skin, and moist skin.

The hazards of abuse are depressed cardiovascular functioning, coma, and death from overdose.

Narcotics come in pill or liquid form. Other signs of use are needles, syringes, and spoons.

Alcohol

More people are addicted to alcohol than to any other chemical in the world. It is also the most fatal addictive substance in the world. Some two hundred thousand alcohol-related deaths occur each year in the United States, compared to six hundred deaths related to cocaine.

The appropriate medical name of this drug is ethyl alcohol.

Among the street names are: beer, wine, whiskey, rye, brandy, scotch, booze, drink, shot, hooch, juice, brew, taste, mountain dew, firewater, highball, cocktail, liquor, moonshine, white lightning.

The method of use is drinking in liquid form.

The symptoms of use are staggering gait, impaired judgment, poor muscle coordination, slurred speech, relaxed inhibitions, poor depth perception, slow reflexes, intoxication, nausea, vomiting, blackouts (drug-induced amnesia), slowed breathing, and decreased sexual performance.

The hazards of use include liver disease, severe withdrawal symptoms (including delirium tremens, shakes, esophageal hemorrhage, elevated blood pressure, and auditory/visual hallucinations), heart failure, respiratory failure, blackouts, progressive memory loss, brain damage, and violent behavior.

The evidence of use is usually beer bottles (or cans), alcohol and wine bottles, and hangovers (bloodshot eyes, headache, upset stomach, shakes, and impaired thinking).

Stimulant or Depressant

This class of drug represents a special case. It is the only drug that may act as either a stimulant or a depressant, depending upon the emotional state of the user. The appropriate medical name is Dexamyl.

The street names of the drug are greenies and copilots.

The medical uses of this drug are for hyperactivity and weight loss.

The symptoms of use may be either excitability or depression.

This drug comes in pill form. It is green in color.

HALLUCINOGENS

Marijuana

The appropriate medical name of this drug is Cannabis.

The street names for it are pot, weed, Acapulco Gold, reefer, Mary Jane, Colombian, Texas tea, grass, Mary J Wanna, joint, rope, roach, Jamaican, and Maui Wowie.

The methods of use are smoking in cigarettes, pipes, or bongs and ingesting in food (especially brownies.)

Medically marijuana is sometimes used in the treatment of glaucoma and—because it powerfully stimulates the appetite—to help cancer patients gain weight. It was once used to treat asthma.

The symptoms of use are a sweet, burnt odor, loss of interest or loss of motivation, weight gain, red or bloodshot eyes, chronic cough, chest pain, impaired concentration/coordination, lethargy, increased appetite, and unkempt appearance.

The hazards of abuse are mood swings, possible damage to the reproductive system, lung disease, emotional retardation, panic reaction, impaired memory, brain damage, and interference with learning. It often leads to addiction to other more powerful drugs.

Evidences of use are marijuana seeds, roaches (the butts of marijuana cigarettes), a bong (a jar with a long hose and mouthpiece for smoking), pipes, cigarette papers, marijuana plant stems, plastic bag with marijuana seeds and/or plant stems, roach clips, and burn holes in shirts, blouses, or other clothing.

A form of marijuana is hashish, which is five to ten times stronger than marijuana. It is known by the street names charas, ganja, bhang, Sinsemilla-hash, hash, Lebanese blonde, cheese, or hash oil.

A form called red oil of cannabis is up to forty-five times stronger than the typical marijuana cigarette.

Hashish is sometimes ground into a light brown powder and mixed into drinks or candies, or laced into marijuana cigarettes to increase their potency.

PCP

The appropriate medical names for this drug are Phencyclidine and Sernyl. It was originally developed as an animal tranquilizer.

The street names for the drug are angel dust, super grass, hog, killer weed, and peace pill.

The most common method of using PCP is smoking. It is usually laced into marijuana cigarettes. It can also be snorted or swallowed.

The symptoms of use include blurred vision, agitation, confusion, uncoordination, slurred speech, panic, nausea, and a mixing of the senses (such as being able to hear colors or smell music. This is not to be confused with the "sixth sense" that some people have naturally, which is a blending of the senses called *synesthesia*).

The hazards of use include extreme anxiety or depression or both, impaired memory, chronic perceptual difficulties, accident proneness, extreme aggressive tendencies that sometimes result in homicide, and death from overdose.

The drug may be found in capsules, tablets, or powder.

LSD

The appropriate medical name of this drug is Lysergic Acid Diethylamine.

The street names for it are acid, cubes, pearly gates, wedding bells, zen, business man's trip, purple haze, mirodot, window pane, orange sunshine, vitamin A, blotter, and orange barrels.

The most common method of use is ingestion of a drop placed on a sugar cube. It can also be injected, swallowed in tablets, or skin-popped (held against the skin until absorbed).

There is no known medical use for this drug.

The symptoms of use include dilated pupils, hallucinations, mood swings, illusions, loss of touch with reality, depression, increased pulse rate, confusion, euphoria, trancelike states, tremors, seeing faces in objects, seeing things as larger or smaller than they are, seeing people with halos, intensification of colors, flashes of color, and afterimages of objects.

The hazards of use include loss of touch with reality that is sometimes permanent, flashbacks, emotional breakdown, and permanent brain damage.

Evidences of use include discovery of the chemical in pill, liquid, or blotter-square form. It may also be found absorbed in sugar cubes or cartoon character tattoos.

Mescaline

The medical name of this drug is Peyote.

The street names are peyote, mesc, cactus buttons, and Yanqui adventure.

The most common method of use is eating in its natural form. It can also be found in powder form.

The symptoms of use are hallucinations, mood swings, wide pupils, loss of touch with reality, trancelike state, euphoria, increased pulse rate, and confusion.

The hazards of use are emotional breakdown and brain damage.

The strongest evidence of mescaline usage, besides the above symptoms, is physical evidence of cactus buttons.

Psilocybin

The medical name is Psilocybin.

The street names of the drug are: magic mushroom, red tops, schrooms, toadstools, and Alice in wonderland.

The most common form of use is eating in its natural form.

Psilocybin has no known medical uses.

The symptoms of use are mood swings, hallucinations, illusions, dilated pupils, and loss of touch with reality.

The hazards of use include emotional breakdown that may be permanent and brain damage.

The evidence of use, other than the above symptoms, is discovery of the fungus itself.

Organic Solvents

Inhalants are found in many forms, including aerosol products such as spray paint and hair spray, and volatile solvents such as gasoline, antifreeze, lighter fluid, transmission fluid, airplane glue, nail polish remover, typewriter correction fluid, vegetable cooking sprays, and paint thinner.

Among street names for these products are bolt snapper, whippits, laughing gas, Pam, glue, rush, locker room, and White-Out.

Methods of use of aerosol products are inhaling the spray directly from the can or spraying its contents into a paper bag and then inhaling. Volatile solvents are inhaled directly from the container; poured into a beer or soda pop can and inhaled, or poured into a cloth that is placed over the user's nose and mouth and inhaled ("huffing").

The symptoms of use are impaired coordination, judgment, vision, and memory; dizziness, headache, loss of bowel or bladder control, fatigue, and nausea.

The hazards of use are irrevocable liver, brain, and blood damage.

Evidences of use include rags, cans, dried glue on face, and odor of chemicals on breath.

COMMONLY ASKED QUESTIONS

Question: I think my mother uses more than one drug. Could she be addicted to both of them?

Answer: Yes. In fact, about half of all addicts are addicted to more than one drug. It is called *polyaddiction.*

Question: I know that some addicts have a favorite drug. When they can't get that, will they use a similar acting drug?

Answer: Yes, the favorite drug is referred to as the *drug of choice.* When that drug is unavailable, they will use one that is similar. For instance, a person who uses crystal will use crack when crystal is unavailable.

Question: My dad seems to use two very different kinds of drugs. Could he be addicted to drugs that are different or even opposite to each other?"

Answer: Yes. Dual addiction is quite common. An example is the person who uses depressants to control anxiety and stimulants to control the depression. One gets him up, the other gets him down.

The Addictive Cycle

Every addict experiences certain drug-induced changes in mood. These mood swings follow a predictable pattern. However, each addict behaves differently depending on the drug or combination of drugs that he uses. The basic addictive cycle goes like this:

1. Pain-relieving use of a chemical or performance of a pain-relieving act.
2. Guilt or loss of self-esteem.
3. Experience of emotional pain, which could be depression, anxiety, or intense boredom.
4. Obsessive thinking about, using, or acting out.
5. Use of a pain-relieving chemical or performance of a pain-relieving act.

It looks like this:

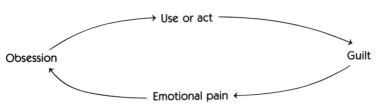

An addict behaves differently depending on where he is in the addictive cycle. That can be very confusing to friends and family. Each of the stages in the addictive cycle impacts everyone who is involved with the user.

The Downer Cycle

People who abuse downers (barbiturates, alcohol, narcotics, etc.) follow this same pattern, but they are in a very distinct kind of emotional pain when they are not using. They feel anxious. For them, the addictive cycle looks like this:

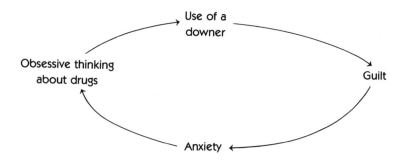

Case Study: Martin's father was an addict. Martin was never quite sure how he would react to anything. But there were times when he was very generous. He bought his son gifts, gave him lots of spending money, took him places, even invited his friends to the movies and paid their way.

Martin didn't realize that at these times his father was recovering from using drugs and feeling guilty about it.

At other times asking for a couple of dollars for something he needed for school would make Dad lash out angrily. These reactions were tied to anxiety.

At still other times Dad would be remote, distant, not quite seeming to see or hear him. At those times Dad had drugs on his mind, and shortly afterward he would be gone for a couple of days. When he came home, he would give Martin anything he wanted and some things he didn't even ask for.

Martin, like most children of addicts, lived in a world of emotional Russian roulette.

The Upper Cycle

The primary difference between addiction to uppers (speed, crystal, crank, cocaine, crack) and downers is that the downer addict is anxious when he isn't using whereas the upper addict is depressed when he isn't using. The behavior of the upper user is very confusing to friends and family. The upper cycle looks like this:

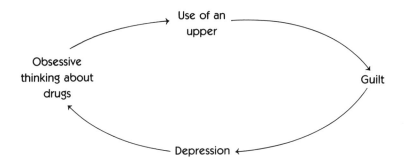

Case Study: Kelly's mother was a speed freak, addicted to crank. Kelly knew she used drugs but didn't understand why she was so mean sometimes. When her mom was using she talked nonstop and was always moving. "Being around her makes you feel sandpapered!" Kelly told a friend. It made her want to grab her mother and scream at her just to hold still and be quiet!

After her mom stopped using she would cry and say how sorry she was and that she was a terrible mother. Kelly would try to console her, but it never seemed to work; no matter what she did, Mom would get worse and worse. She would be quiet and withdrawn, often locking herself in the bedroom and only coming out long enough to eat the meals Kelly cooked.

Then would begin the telephone calls to her dealer and other drug-using friends, the efforts to get together enough money for more crank. Kelly dreaded those times. When Mom reached that point she was hostile and sarcastic, sometimes slapping or punching Kelly without reason or justification. During those times Kelly was very afraid of her.

The Upper/Downer Cycle

This cycle can be extremely confusing to the child of an addict. The upper/downer cycle happens when a person is dually addicted. The addict uses one chemical to get up and another to get down. The cycle looks like this:

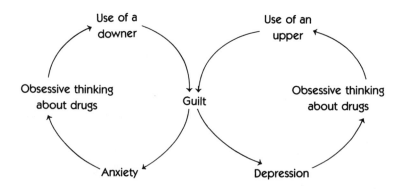

As can be seen from the diagram, the person addicted to uppers and downers is predictably unpredictable. His family and friends can never be certain where he is on the cycle. They can never be certain whether guilt will be followed by use of an upper or a downer, or whether the person will be depressed or anxious later.

What makes it even more confusing is that sometimes when addicts are down (after using a downer) they seem happy, and at other times when they are down (when they are depressed) they are miserable. The same is true for those times when they are up. Sometimes (after using uppers) they are frenetic, always moving, bionic-mouthed talkers, and sometimes (coming up after using a downer) they are extremely anxious and angry. No one has any idea what to expect.

Case Study: Charlotte's mother was addicted to crystal and Quaaludes. She felt certain she needed both drugs just to survive, to get through each day. One day Charlotte found her mother curled up and sobbing in a corner of the living room. Charlotte sat down with her, tried to cheer her up, told her everything was going to be fine, but Mom hardly seemed to hear her. She seemed remote, unreachable.

A week later Charlotte found her mother in the same corner, seeming depressed but also at peace. She was singing, over and over, an old song called "Mellow Yellow."

The next day Mom was angry and agitated. When Charlotte tried to understand what was going on, Mom slapped her viciously and began screaming at her.

But two days later Mom wanted to talk. In fact, she sat in Charlotte's room talking until 4 a.m., even though Charlotte had two tests the next day at school. Mom wasn't making a lot of sense, but she was talking!

To her boyfriend, Charlotte described her life at home as "a roller coaster through hell."

The Hallucinogen Cycle

People who use hallucinogens (PCP, LSD, peyote, mushroom) are a special case. Their cycle has some very different components. That is especially true if the person actually uses in the presence of family members because of the unreal things a hallucinogen causes the user to see, hear, and smell.

It is not unusual for a user to think that he or she can fly, to carry on a conversation with a person who is dead, or to believe snakes have invaded the house.

One use may cause pleasant delusions such as having sex or seeing beautiful colors; the next use may cause fearful delusions such as being attacked by a monster or seeing blood everywhere.

One of the scariest things about these drugs is that a flashback can happen at any time. A flashback is a reexperience of a drug trip, good or bad, when the addict is not using. It can be very dangerous.

Imagine that a parent has a flashback when driving a car on a busy interstate highway. All of a sudden he is seeing rivers of beautiful colors. His children can't understand what is happening. All they know is that the car is out of control and Dad seems very happy.

The hallucinogen cycle looks like this:

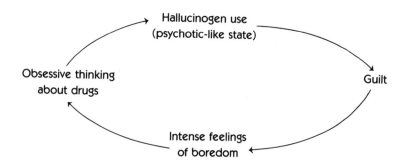

Because of the powerful action of hallucinogens on the brain, users are completely unpredictable. That is especially true during flashbacks. The content of a flashback experience is also unpredictable.

Case Study: Ginny and her family were finally going on vacation. Everybody was happy and excited, all of them were in the van with Mom driving down Interstate 10. In less than two hours they would be at Grandmother's house.

Dad seemed to be half asleep when all of a sudden he began lashing out and screaming, "Leave me alone! Leave me alone!" although no one was near him or had touched him or even spoken to him. Before anyone could stop him, he opened the door and jumped out of the van.

By the time Mom got stopped and everybody ran back to find Dad, several vehicles had run over him. An autopsy found nothing to explain what had happened. But after the funeral Dad's brother revealed that he had been a heavy user of LSD in college, fifteen years ago.

LIVING WITH AN ADDICTED PARENT

As mentioned earlier, most addicts lead lives that are outwardly fairly normal. People who know them often have no idea that they have a problem.

But for family members that problem dominates their lives.

The word most used by the children of addicts to describe their lives is uncertainty. They never know from one minute to the next how Mom is going to act, what Dad is going to do.

When they get up in the morning, will Dad smile and say "Good morning"? Or will he backhand them because they smile and say "Good morning"? When they come home from school, will Mom be in the kitchen baking cookies, or will she be passed out on the living room floor? Will they have money to go to the game as promised, or will it all have been spent on crack? Will Dad come home tonight, or will they get a call that he is in jail, or the hospital, or the morgue?

Will they have a home to come home to much longer? Dad has been having job problems because of his drinking, and if he is fired . . .

Cory, fifteen, put it very well. "You just never have any idea what to expect. You learn not to get your hopes up for anything. You also learn never to trust what they say, or any promises they make. You take it all with, 'Yeah, I'll believe it when I see it, okay?'"

In most families a lot of effort is put into concealment, denial, "putting up a front," so that outsiders will not know that anything is wrong.

There is often a great deal of isolation. Children are not encouraged to have friends come over—they might see Dad crocked or realize that the smoke in the kitchen where Mom is didn't come from burned biscuits. Often children are restricted in their attempts to form other friendships or have a social life outside the home, lest they "let something slip."

Money is often a real problem, even though the family may appear to be affluent.

As the daughter of one addict put it, "Nobody can understand why I don't have money for a lot of things at school and don't have nice clothes when we live in an expensive house and Dad's an executive with his company. They don't know how much money goes up his and Mom's nose. I heard her tell him once that they'd spent almost $1,000 for cocaine in *one week*! Yet they couldn't come up with enough money for me to have a pep squad uniform.

People look shocked when I say I hate my parents, but I do. I really do!"

Physical or sexual abuse or both are much more likely to happen to children. Even though a parent may have been violent only once or twice, or perhaps never has been violent, family members usually feel that the potential is always there. The son of one alcoholic, who had only been hit twice while his father was drunk, said, "I know he could always lose control again. It's like walking on eggs, the way you feel you have to act around him."

If other parents knew about your parent's addiction, they might hold it against *you*, for example not allowing a son or daughter to go out with you or go to your house.

Family members are put into roles (more about that in Chapter 8). Almost no one is allowed to be himself or herself, to be the kind of person he or she would be in a family that did not have a problem.

Sometimes the roles in the family are reversed, with you being given, or taking on, the job of taking care of and being responsible for a parent, instead of the other way around.

Almost universally, say the children of addicted parents, it robs you of your childhood. You will not have childhood memories like other people. Your childhood has been lost trying to cope with a parent's addiction.

CHAPTER ◇ 4

Addiction as a

Disease

For centuries it was thought that addiction came about
because of a person's inborn sinful nature. Addicts
were seen as having a basic problem with willpower.
In other words, they were evil and could not control their
evil impulses.

Recently, however, that has changed. In 1956 the
American Medical Association referred to addiction and
alcoholism as a disease, and today it is so classified both
medically and legally.

Social workers, psychologists, marriage and family ther-
apists, and drug and alcohol counselors today refer to and
treat addiction as a disease.

The term *disease* has been defined in several ways:

1. A pathological (unhealthy) syndrome (condition)
   possessing a group or set of concurrent symptoms
   (several symptoms at the same time).
2. An abnormal condition of an organ, or part,

especially as a consequence of infection, inherent weakness, or environmental stress, that impairs normal functioning.

3. A pathological state that has a known etiology (cause), a predictable course, and a definite outcome.

It makes little difference which of these definitions you use. It is clear that alcohol or drug addiction fits all of them.

We know that drug addiction is "a pathological syndrome possessing a set of concurrent symptoms." We also know that it is "an abnormal condition as a consequence of inherent weakness (see discussion of THIQ in Chapter 1) that impairs normal functioning."

This chapter is largely concerned with describing the "known etiology, predictable course, and definite outcome" mentioned in definition three.

A Known Etiology

Etiology means cause. The cause was described in Chapter 1. Persons become addicted because they have inherited a genetic predisposition to create THIQ in their brain.

A Predictable Course

That means that the addiction will follow a certain pattern in all persons. This course expresses itself in three definite stages: Chemical (early), Behavioral (middle), and Chronic (late).

Early Stage—Chemical

1. First sign: increased tolerance of alcohol or drugs.
2. Has blackouts (not everyone has them).

3. Sneaks drinks or drugs.
4. Is preoccupied with drinking or drugs.
5. Uses alcohol or drugs to relieve anxiety.
6. Avoids references to addiction.
7. Is uncomfortable in situations without drugs or alcohol.
8. Loses control.
9. Needs to use before or after social occasions.

Middle Stage—Behavior

10. Is dishonest about the way he or she uses alcohol or drugs.
11. Invents alibis.
12. Tries to control use of alcohol or drugs.
13. Reproves self.
14. Drinks or uses drugs alone or secretly.
15. First drink or drug use becomes urgent.
16. Shows extravagance.
17. Readily shows jealousy and is sometimes unreasonable.
18. Experiences decrease in sexual capacity.
19. Exhibits aggression.
20. Neglects eating.
21. Attempts to stop using from time to time.
22. Feels remorse.
23. Incurs disapproval of family and associates.
24. Rationalizes and excuses use of alcohol or drugs.
25. Changes pattern of use.
26. Social life decays.
27. Has family difficulties.
28. Has problems on job.
29. Seeks help.
30. Accumulates a list of resentments.

31. Attempts a geographical solution by moving.
32. Maintains and protects supply.
33. Has episodes of chain drinking or using.
34. Undergoes physical and psychological changes.

Late Stage—Chronic

35. Engages in early-morning use of alcohol or drugs.
36. Undergoes moral deterioration.
37. Has chronic health problems.
38. Experiences persistent and unyielding grief.
39. Undergoes hospitalization.
40. Nuclear family breaks down.
41. Excuses are overworked.
42. Thinking becomes illogical.
43. Goes on binges for longer periods of time.
44. Working becomes impossible.
45. Experiences intense jealousies.
46. Uses with increasingly lower social classes.
47. Thinking is impaired.
48. Tolerance decreases.
49. Suffers undefinable fears.
50. Has tremors and shakes.
51. Develops psychomotor inhibitions (physical impairment of, for example, hand-eye coordination).
52. Resorts to religious consumption (praying to keep a drink down).
53. Death.
Note: No one addict has all symptoms.

A Definite Outcome

Unfortunately, all drug addiction that is allowed to run its course unchecked is fatal.

All untreated drug addicts and alcoholics die prematurely from physical illness, suicide, or accident—all associated with their addiction. The statistics speak for themselves. Alcohol or drugs are involved in:

45% of all nonaccident hospital admissions
50% of all fatal traffic accidents
33% of all suicides
86% of all fire fatalities
65% of all drownings
70% of all fatal falls

The Addicted
Personality

People who are addicted tend to use very specific defense mechanisms to deal with the emotional pain of being addicted. Those defenses are: denial, projection, minimization, displacement, blaming, expressions of anger, repression of feelings, blackouts with confabulation, and rigidity.

Denial

Denial is defined as the psychological process of not knowing the extent of one's own addiction. Those who are addicted to a mood-altering chemical do not know how much of the chemical they use or how frequently they use it.

Case Study: Rose's mother was an alcoholic. She was rarely at home when Rose came in from school. This afternoon was no different. As soon as she entered the house Rose noticed the beer cans on the coffee table, the couch, and the floor. She picked them up and took them to the trash can in the kitchen.

The next afternoon Rose went with her mother to keep an appointment with the doctor, who seemed very concerned about her.

He asked a question that Rose couldn't quite hear, but her mother's answer was clear: "Yes, I drink a beer now and then."

The doctor asked, "How many do you drink?"

"Never more than two or three."

Rose stared in astonishment. "But Mom, yesterday you drank at least twenty before you went out. I know—I put the cans in the trash!"

Now it was her mother's turn to stare. "Whatever are you talking about, honey? I don't drink twenty cans of beer a year!"

Projection

Projection is defined as subconsciously transferring emotional pain to another person. When projection is used to deal with pain, the addict does not experience his own pain. He believes that it belongs to someone else.

Case Study: Carol's father came home from work early one day. Carol was very surprised, because he was usually late, stopping off at bars on the way home.

She asked, "What are you doing home so early?"

"I got laid off," her father replied calmly.

"Oh, Dad, how awful! Are you okay? I mean, is everything all right?"

"It's okay. And I'm all right. But you should have seen how upset my secretary was! And poor Mr. Johnson, I thought he was going to start crying when he told me he had to let me go!"

Minimization

Minimization is the psychological defense of grossly underrating the importance of certain events.

Case Study: Stanley and Bruno were playing on the school grounds at recess when they saw a police car pull up in front of the school. Bruno said, "Wow! Stan, that's your dad in that cop car. What's going on?"

Wide-eyed, Stanley said, "I don't know, but it looks like Mom's in there and they're looking for me." Both boys began to run.

"Dad, what's going on? Is something wrong?"

"I guess so. That mother of yours, always smoking in bed! Now she's burned the house down!"

Stanley knew that Mom also drank in bed and that his parents were always fighting about it. Now he began to cry. "Dad, that's awful! Where will we live?"

"Look, it's no big deal," his mother said, getting unsteadily out of the police car. "We needed a new house anyway."

Stanley could tell that his father was very upset, but his mother just staggered a little as she walked up to the fence. "What's all the fuss about, anyway?"

Displacement

Displacement is taking out your anger on someone other than the person with whom you are angry.

Case Study: Darrel's father had had a bad afternoon at

work. During lunch he had slipped away to smoke a couple of marijuana cigarettes, and during the afternoon he was more often chatting with coworkers or blundering around running into things than really doing his job. Just before quitting time he got a royal chewing-out by the foreman and was told that unless his job performance improved he would be fired.

He was furious with the foreman but didn't dare do anything but stand there and say, "Yes, sir," "No, sir." But the minute he got home that evening he began to scream at Darrel for having things scattered on the dining room table (Darrel was doing his homework), and at his wife because dinner wasn't ready (he had said he was going to take them out for pizza that night.)

He didn't dare hit back at the foreman, but Darrel and his mother were "safe" targets for his temper.

The children of addicts are the subjects of a lot of displaced anger.

Blaming

Blaming is the psychological defense of holding someone else responsible for one's own behavior.

Case Study: Gretchen's mother was really stoned out of her mind when she came in that evening, and her dad was furious. He bellowed, "You've blown your paycheck on cocaine again, damn you! You're nothing but a coke-head, and that's all you'll ever be! My mother was right about you! You'll never amount to anything and you'll never quit!"

Her mother began to scream back, "Oh, really! You want to know why I need to use coke? Look in the mirror, you wimp! It's all your fault. You and that damned daughter of yours. I wouldn't need it if it weren't for the two of you, hanging on me, wanting this and that . . . It's not *my* fault. I'm an innocent victim of circumstances."

Sure.

Repression of Feelings

This is a self-explanatory psychological defense. Addicts operate somewhat like robots. They experience few emotions, because they typically repress their feelings.

Case Study: Celia's father was coming down from using speed, and to her he seemed pretty depressed. She wasn't sure whether it was because of the drugs or because his mother had just passed away and they had always been close. Celia decided to try to comfort him. He was sitting on the couch, just staring at the wall, and he seemed so alone.

She sat down beside him and said, "I love you, Dad, and I'm so sorry about Grandmother. I bet you miss her a lot."

"Not really," her father said, remotely. "She never really knew me. I guess she was all right."

Then he got up and left. Somehow Celia knew he was going after more speed.

Expression of Anger

Anger is usually the only feeling that is expressed freely by an addicted person.

Case Study: Adam's father is a binge alcoholic. He isn't always drunk, but he *is* always angry. Adam can barely remember a normal conversation with his father. Most attempts to talk end up with Dad yelling at the top of his lungs. Most of the time Adam just avoids his father when that is possible.

Most of the family avoids him, too, so Dad has taken his anger outside and spends a lot of his time picking fights with the neighbors. He threatened to shoot a neighbor's dog that got out and was playing on his lawn. When the fat woman across the street works in her front yard, he yells insults. He called the police because smoke from the next-door neighbor's grill was coming into his backyard. Once Adam heard the neighbors on each side joking about going halves on a hit man.

Adam used to get along well with the people in the neighborhood, but now everyone is so disgusted with his father that they are beginning to act as if they don't want *him* around.

Blackouts with Confabulation

A blackout is a period of amnesia, of being unable to remember the events of a certain period of time. Blackouts occur because of excessive use of mood-altering chemicals. They can occur at any time, even when the addict is sober or not on drugs.

Confabulation is a psychological defense against the aftereffects of a blackout. It is filling in the memory gaps with a made-up sequence of events. In other words, the addict invents a version of what happened during the blackout. When that occurs it is very difficult to convince the addict that his version is not the truth.

Case Study: Melissa's dad was in a great mood. She enjoyed it so much when he was like this. They were watching a television special together, and he was funnier than anything on the screen. She laughed until she cried and her side hurt. Then her mother came home from a meeting.

"How'd the evening go?" she asked.

Melissa's father replied, "Okay, I guess. I watched TV for a while, and Melissa was upstairs in her room."

Astonished, Melissa stared at him and said, "But, Dad, I was right here with you, watching TV, too!"

"Don't be ridiculous," her father snapped. "I've hardly seen you this evening and after I stayed here especially to watch TV with you. You act as if everything else comes before the family. See if I make another effort to spend time with you!" and he slammed the door as he left the room.

"Mom, Mom!" Melissa cried, "I was right here!"

Melissa's mother glared at her. "You could give some time to your dad. All you ever think about is yourself."

Melissa went slowly up to her room, wondering if she were going insane.

Rigidity

Rigidity is defined as the disallowing of new ways of thinking. The addicted person typically rejects new ideas, new ways of doing or thinking about anything.

Case Study: Paul's father was addicted to marijuana and, Paul thought, also used other drugs from time to time. He was a plumber whose job it was to install gas lines between butane tanks and houses. One summer Paul agreed to work with his father. Although Dad would not admit it, Paul could see that he was falling further and further behind in his work, and his boss was becoming more and more impatient with him.

Recently he had threatened to fire him. Paul was

determined to help—that was something all the family were afraid might happen.

When they arrived at the job site early in the morning Paul grabbed a pick and shovel and shouted, "I'll dig this one, you dig that one." He finished his ditch in about twenty minutes and ran back to where his father was toiling away. "I'm through," he said.

His father scowled and snapped, "Bull! You couldn't possibly be through."

Then Paul looked at the ditch his father was digging. It was only about a fourth done, but it had straight sides and a flat bottom, and Paul knew that his father wasn't going to like his ditch.

"Let's see," his dad said, and walked to where Paul had been working. Sure enough, he didn't like it. He began to shout, "That's not how you dig a ditch! A ditch has *straight* sides and a *flat* bottom. Get back in there and get to work!"

"But Dad," Paul protested, "We're just going to lay a gas line in it and cover it up again, aren't we? What does it matter what the thing *looks* like?"

His father ignored that and kept screaming at him for not knowing how to dig a ditch and being lazy on top of that. Paul shrugged and went back to work and eventually gave the ditch straight sides and a flat bottom. But during lunch he noticed that another man on the crew, a guy named John, had dug a ditch just like Paul's, and the boss walked by and looked approving.

Two days later Paul's father was fired. Paul heard him complaining to his mother, "He has given John more hours, and John doesn't even know how to dig a ditch, not to mention lay pipe."

Paul's father's thinking was so locked into digging a ditch the way *he* thought it should be that he didn't even notice that his work was much too slow and he wasted a lot of time. When the boss tried to point that out to him, he argued about it.

"WHAT CAN *I* DO ABOUT A PARENT'S ADDICTION/ALCOHOLISM?"

Unfortunately, probably not very much.

You may have heard, and it is certainly true, that addicts can change only when *they* want to change. Almost never can they be bullied, reasoned with, shamed, made to feel guilty, or emotionally blackmailed into trying to break free of addiction.

Unhappily, family members seldom realize that, or realize it in time to save themselves a lot of anguish.

A child's efforts to get a parent to stop drinking or using can run a wide range: "Don't you love us enough to stop hurting us like this?" "Dad, you could quit if you wanted to. People quit all the time. Please do it for us!" "You don't care about us! Geting high on coke is all in this world that matters to you!" "Driving drunk like that, you are going to have a wreck and kill someone. How will you feel then?" "Mom, if you didn't love us enough to take care of us like a real mother, why did you have us in the first place?" "Dad, did you know Bob has started drinking after school whenever he can get liquor, and it seems like he always can. He's going to be just like you, you know that?"

Probably every argument in the world has been tried by the children of addicts and alcoholics as they try frantically to find the right button that will send Mom or Dad to get help and break free.

When nothing works, the child too often thinks it is his fault, that somehow he or she should have been able to find the magic key that would make Mom or Dad suddenly decide to change.

Actually, strenuous efforts on the part of a child can make the situation worse, not better, at least in some cases. The addicted parent interprets it as nagging (which it is). Most people, when nagged, tend to simply dig in their heels and become even more stubbornly determined not to do whatever someone is trying to get them to do.

An addicted parent may think, or say out loud, "Blasted kid! What does he mean, I drink too much? I don't drink too much, and I resent his saying it. If he thinks he can make me give up a few relaxing drinks in the evening he's got another think coming." Or, "Little miss smartie pants! Who does she think she is, trying to run my life? I'll show her!" Or some other version that basically means, "He can talk until he's blue in the face. I don't intend to change one little bit."

Case Study: Ryan's father had always been a heavy drinker, but in the last two or three years Ryan had realized that the drinking was out of control and that his father passed out in a sodden stupor almost every weekend.

Ryan began by trying to get his father interested in the things he used to like—playing football or softball with Ryan and some of the neighborhood guys. Dad wasn't interested and became angry when Ryan pressed the issue.

Then Ryan tried pleading. "Come on, Dad, do it for us. We love you, and we worry about you." Total effect on Dad, zero. Zilch. Goose egg.

Next up was guilt. "Mom's worried about the money you spend on booze and the time you lose from work. What's going to happen to us if you get fired? We'll wind up homeless, like the people you see on TV!"

The more Ryan tried, the more angry and abusive his father became, until one night he backhanded Ryan through a glass patio door, which shattered, cutting him badly in several places. Stunned and bleeding, Ryan lay in the sea of broken glass as his father ranted and raved about what an awful son he was.

In the hospital Ryan finally told the doctor the whole story. The doctor recommended Alateen, the division of Alcoholics Anonymous for young people.

"But Dad won't go. I couldn't make him go. I've failed . . ."

"Son, you don't go to their meetings for your dad. You go for yourself. It's to help *you* cope with your dad's drinking problem."

At Alateen Ryan heard from other young people like himself about their efforts to make a parent stop drinking, and how they too felt guilty and like failures when they were unable to change him or her.

Oddly enough, as Ryan formed new friendships within the group, became active in some of their projects, and got on with his life, his father began to realize that Ryan didn't seem to care anymore what happened, or at least not the way he once had. Realization penetrated his father's alcoholic haze that he was losing the son he really loved.

Eventually he joined Alcoholics Anonymous and did stop drinking.

Happy endings like that don't always happen, and certainly that had not been what the doctor had in mind when he recommended Alateen nor what Ryan had hoped for when he first joined. All he knew was that if he had gone on trying to get his father to stop, it almost certainly would never have happened.

A child cannot change addicted parents in 999.99 times out of a thousand. Don't let yourself be drawn into feeling guilty or sad or depressed because of that. Get help for yourself and go on with your life.

CHAPTER 6

Coaddiction

T he inner workings of a family that contains an addict or addicts are often very confusing to outsiders— *and* to some family members as well. It can best be described as a case of coaddiction.

The coaddict relationship is a *reciprocal relationship that is characterized by one person who behaves in an addicted manner and another who tries to control that person's addictive behavior.*

The following are the most commonly asked questions by those trying to understand the mechanics of coaddiction.

What is a coaddict?

Any person who has lived in an addicted family system could be correctly labeled a coaddict. Everyone in an addicted family system has been affected by the addict's use of a mood-altering drug. And all of them in their own ways make an adaptive response to the addict's behavior. These responses are attempts to control the stress in an extremely painful family situation.

In a more specific way, the spouse of an addict is the person in the family system who is usually identified as the coaddict.

Do coaddicts have specific traits by which they can be identified?

Yes. In fact, all coaddicts have a large number of very similar personality traits. They also exhibit characteristic behavior patterns.

It makes little difference whether the coaddict is a child or an adult, a parent or a stepparent. Coaddiction is not dependent upon the addict's drug of choice.

What are the traits of a coaddict?

The coaddict has weak interpersonal boundaries, is dependent, denies the reality of his situation, is controlling, is obsessed, has low self-worth, practices caretaking, is overly rigid, does not stand up for himself, and does not leave the relationship when it is clear that the addict is violating the coaddict's values and has no intention of trying to change.

What are "weak interpersonal boundaries"?

Boundaries are the limits a person has set on his own or another person's behavior. Boundaries are of two types: personal and interpersonal. A personal boundary might be a decision never to participate in an extramarital affair. An interpersonal boundary might be a decision never to stay married to a spouse who is having an extramarital affair.

A personal boundary might be that you would probably keep money you found in the street but that you would never steal. An interpersonal boundary might be that you would not date or stay friends with a person who would steal.

Coaddicts often say that they would never tolerate a certain behavior, such as excessive drinking or the use of drugs, by another person. Yet when the other person exhibits that behavior, the coaddict stays in the relationship anyway.

Case Study: Renee's father is heavily into the use of cocaine. Her mother is always covering up for him, telling the boss he is sick, making excuses, and so on. Renee despises them both for the way they are acting and what they are doing to each other's lives and the lives of her little brother and sister and herself.

Yet much the same situation is occurring in Renee's own life. Her friend Karin is putting her to the test about stealing. Renee would never steal anything, yet over and over after they had been shopping Renee would realize that Karin had been shoplifting. Renee said angrily that she did not want Karin to steal while they were in a store together. Yet two weeks later she saw Karin slipping a tube of mascara into her purse. Outside, Renee shouted furiously on her friend. Karin was upset and embarrassed and promised never to do it again.

Within days Renee once again saw Karin stealing, slipping a bottle of perfume into a pocket. This time she told Karin point-blank that she would no longer be her friend if Karin continued to steal things, no matter how small. Karin swore she would never do it again.

But before another week had passed Renee saw Karin slip a piece of jewelry into her purse. This time Renee said nothing.

While she hated the way her mother made things easy

for her father in his addiction, she was slipping into exactly the same behavior pattern with her friend.

What does "dependent" mean?

The dependent person has an inadequate sense of self. He or she seeks approval from others instead of making his or her own decisions. The dependent stays in relationships that don't work, that may even hurt. He or she is terrified of being abandoned and frequently allows others to abuse him or her. He puts his life on hold for other people.

Women and girls who believe that "You are nothing without a man," that it takes a man to "complete" you or your life, or who accept the words of a song popular in the '60s, "You're nobody 'til somebody loves you . . . " are mostly likely to be strongly dependent and to be hurt by that clinging dependence on someone else. But men can be dependent too.

Case Study: William's wife was characterized as "having a tongue that could clip a hedge," and Susie frequently turned her caustic comments on her husband, especially when she had been drinking. And that was often. Four to five nights a week she came home drunk, calling William ugly names.

William never answered back. He was afraid that if he made her angry she would leave him. He would be abandoned.

Late one Saturday night Susie came home so drunk that she couldn't get her key in the lock. William heard her stabbing at the door and cursing, so he opened the door for her.

"I've been worried about you," he said mildly. "I was afraid you might have been hurt in a car accident."

Susie focused on him blearily and said, "You poor, poor pitiful man. You have nothing more important to do than wring your hands and worry about me. What would you ever do if you had to live by yourself?"

William didn't answer but just stood looking cowed. He had tears in his eyes, but he didn't respond to his wife's acidity.

"If you were any kind of a man, I wouldn't need to drink. I think I'll just go back to the bar. At least there are intelligent people there to talk to, not a sniveling little wimp."

"Please," begged William, "you've had too much to drink to be able to drive."

His wife just sneered as she staggered back to her car. William went back into the house without another word.

Often, and frequently without being aware that they are doing it, dependent people *encourage* addictive or other destructive behavior in a spouse. They reason: "If he really drinks too much, I can help protect him from the consequences. He will *need* me. That way he'll never want to leave."

Or, "I really wish my wife would lose some weight. But if she did she might be attractive enough to other men that one would take her away from me, and I couldn't stand that. She's so happy with this new diet—think I'll go out and get her a giantpizza and some ice cream. I'll tell her just once won't hurt."

That explains, to some degree, the situation that so many children of addicts see and find so confusing: On the one hand Mom is always after Dad to quit drinking so much and complains about what his drinking is doing to all of them. Yet on the other hand for his birthday she buys him a fancy decanter of very expensive whiskey.

How do coaddicts deny the reality of their situation?

Coaddicts become very good at denying many things. They deny that their "significant other"—a boyfriend or girlfriend or a spouse—is addicted. They deny that their children are being abused. They deny that they are unhappy, that they themselves have been abused.

They deny that they have feelings. They deny the embarrassment caused by their spouse's addiction. They deny that the spouse's addiction is tearing the family apart, leaving their children with deep emotional scars.

Case Study: Reginald's wife is an addict, addicted to alcohol, occasionally using drugs. She is frequently abusive to their children, once breaking the youngest girl's arm when she threw her against a wall in an alcoholic rage. She is frequently hostile to Reginald and sometimes attacks him physically.

Yet to outsiders Reginald says things like, "This has been a truly great year. The Lord has blessed us abundantly. He has given me a good wife and great children. And it is remarkable how well we get along together."

Reginald has just made this speech to the Sunday School class he teaches. As they leave the classroom one of his friends says to Reginald, "You really are lucky to have a family that gets along. In my family we fight over trivial matters far too often. I wish we didn't fight as much as we do. It sure would make life better."

Reginald didn't see his son walking behind him as he replied, "That really is a shame. I wish there were a way I could help you and your family get along better. My wife and I used to fight sometimes, but we stopped that years ago."

Reggie Jr. is thunderstruck. The fight that had erupted

between his parents the previous night ended with Mom bopping Dad over the head with a skillet and himself getting knocked over a chair when he tried to break it up. His back and ribs still hurt. Mom and Dad had screamed at each other for hours even after they quit hitting.

Reggie Jr. knows he is living in a nightmare, yet hearing his father talk like that and knowing the truth is making him doubt his own perception of what is and is not real.

How are coaddicts controlling?

A coaddict tries to control the addict's drinking or using and generally goes from that to trying to control his life and sometimes the lives of their children. He or she pours out liquor, flushes drugs down the toilet, hides money so that the addict cannot buy more alcohol or drugs.

The coaddict may go on to trying to control most or all aspects of the addict's life so there is no opportunity to buy drugs. If that is impossible, and it generally is, he or she may go on to demand tyrannical control of the children's lives, just to feel in control of *something*.

Case Study: Carmelita's dad is an alcoholic. For the last two or three years her mother has been searching the house every day for liquor and pouring what she finds down the sink. Lately she has taken to driving her husband to work, meeting him for lunch as often as possible, and driving him home at night. She hopes that this way she can keep him from buying liquor.

It isn't working, and her parents are fighting more and more as her dad drinks more and more. Lately Mom has stepped up her efforts to control her family. She calls her husband four or five times a day at work and insists on going with him whenever he leaves the house at night.

All that is bad enough and seems to be making Dad drink more. But lately Mom has begun acting the same way to Carmelita and her brothers, John and Joe. Mom demands to know where they are at all times, whom they are with, what they are doing. Rules have become more rigid, hard and fast.

For example, they are supposed to be home no later than twenty minutes after school is out. One day Carmelita called to say that they were having cheerleader tryouts and she was going to try. Mom interrupted with a furious order to be home in twenty minutes or else.

Rules make the children like prisoners. Carmelita may *not* wear her skirts more than one inch above or below her kneecap. She may not date until she is sixteen, and that means not even walking to the neighborhood movie with the boy next door who is a year younger than she is but a good friend.

Carmelita and her brothers are right—the rules don't make a lot of sense. They are Mom's way of trying to control *some* aspects of a family situation that she correctly sees as getting away from her and heading for a total smash.

What does "caretaking" mean?

Caretaking refers to being overly responsible, doing things for other people that they could and should do for themselves.

Coaddicts are often so overly responsible that they give away opportunities to have their own needs met. They wind up overcommitted, feeling other people's problems more deeply than do the people themselves. They feel more comfortable giving than receiving and offer advice when it is not wanted or needed.

Like the very dependent person, they need to be "needed."

Case Study: Kevin is fourteen. He and his friends were watching television when he suddenly had an attack of the sneezes. His mother, who happened to be walking through the den at precisely that moment, pulled a tissue from a box and wiped Kevin's nose. It embarrassed him a great deal. "Mom," he said, in protest, "I'm old enough to do that myself!"

"I'm sorry—I guess to me you'll always be my little boy."

"Mom, I'm not your little boy! I'm fourteen. Come on, give me a break!"

Kevin's mother's eyes filled with tears. "Nobody seems to want me anymore."

Later Mom asked about Kevin's homework. "Yes, I have some homework," Kevin said, digging it out of his backpack.

"Can I help you with it, honey?"

"Not now. This is easy." Again with tears threatening, Mom went to the kitchen to begin clearing up. But soon she stopped and began to fix Kevin an elaborate snack.

"Here, honey," she said, "I've fixed you something to snack on while you do your homework, since I don't seem to be able to help you any other way."

"Mom, it wasn't necessary. This really isn't hard and won't take long. Besides, we just finished dinner and I'm not hungry. Why are you always doing things for me that I can do for myself? Don't you trust me to be able to take care of myself or know what I want or need?"

Kevin's mother left the room quickly with tears in her eyes. She then decided to find Kevin's sister, Nell, and see how she could take care of her.

What are some examples of obsession?

Coaddicts often worry about minute and unimportant details. They spend much time and energy dealing with other people's problems. They try to catch others doing something wrong. They frequently worry about another's behavior. Sometimes they are unable to sleep worrying about what someone else has done, or might do.

They focus on another person to the point of ignoring things that should be important to themselves.

Case Study: Harold's wife was an alcoholic. He was obsessed with controlling her drinking. He had been taking her to work, having lunch with her, and picking her up after work for over a year. He spent almost every waking moment with her during the weekends.

One night while she was cooking dinner she said to Harold, "We're out of bread, honey, and we need some for dinner."

At this simple statement Harold felt his pulse race. "How will I handle this?" he thought, with something akin to panic. "She can't quit cooking because the boys have to eat. If I cook dinner and she goes to the store, she may stop on the way and buy a bottle. If I leave her here alone while I go to the store, she may drink. I know what to do! I'll mark the level of whiskey in the bottle. That way, I'll know if she takes a drink."

Harold sped to the nearest convenience store, grabbed a loaf of bread, and rushed to the front of the check-out line and dropped two dollars on the counter, saying, "Keep the change!"

He sped home and ran into the house. His wife was calmly at work in the kitchen. He handed her the bread and headed for the den, where he checked the whiskey bottle. Not a drop was missing, and he felt a great sense of relief.

But back in the kitchen he realized that his wife was acting as if she had been drinking. He couldn't figure it out. None of the whiskey was gone, but she sure seemed to have had something to drink.

He began to search the house. No other bottles were to be found. Harold began to wonder if he were losing his mind. What Harold didn't know was that his wife knew about the mark on the whiskey bottle. She had poured a glass of whiskey and drunk it, then carefully filled the bottle to the pencil line with tea.

Harold felt even more obsessed with his wife and her drinking. Now he had to know whether or not he was crazy. That night he couldn't sleep worrying about ways to increase his vigilance.

What Harold had not seen was that his preoccupation with his wife was putting his job at risk, and that his oldest son was smoking marijuana on a steadily increasing basis.

How do codependents fail to stand up for themselves?

They allow others to control their behavior. They allow themselves to be criticized unjustly and frequently play down their own abilities. They allow themselves to be treated unfairly and to be victimized by others.

They are overly judgmental and harsh with themselves, and yet they are also afraid to ask important questions— questions they think might rock the boat. They are too sensitive. Their lives are filled with self-imposed "shoulds" —"I should do this," "I should have done that and I know things would have been better if I'd had the common sense to do it," "Tomorrow, instead of concentrating on my job, I should . . ." And so on and so on. All others' needs come before their own.

Case study: Bill is addicted to speed, although he will use just about any drug he can get this hands on. His marriage is very shaky because of debts, the increasingly shabby dump where the family lives, and his failure to hold a job. This is his second marriage. He has custody of his son, Mark.

According to Bill, all their problems are the fault of his wife, Susan. When he missed a date with his connection to buy drugs and began to go into withdrawal, he was furious with Susan. He screamed at her because she had taken the car to apply for a job and was gone an hour and a half. Instead of replying, "The big boss wanted to talk to me. I couldn't very well walk out if I wanted the job, could I?" Susan said nothing.

When he blamed their bills and debts on her "wild spending" (she had just spent $30 on much needed new clothes for the new job), she didn't point out that he was spending hundreds a week on drugs.

In fact, she did blame herself, certain that if she had been "a good wife" Bill wouldn't act as he did and would be able to kick his habit.

Finally she began to see, and tried to point out to Bill, that Mark was beginning to act just like his father. Nothing that went wrong in his life was his fault. He could always blame someone else.

One morning Bill and Mark woke up and found Susan gone. After five years of browbeating and failure to take up for herself, Susan had realized it was time, and past time, to split.

How can a coaddict know when it is time to leave a relationship?

It is important for a coaddict to decide what he or she is willing to live with and what his or her bottom line is. Once those things are decided, he or she should be willing to take action according to that bottom line. That could include leaving the relationship, as Susan did.

Case Study: Cybil was in the kitchen one day when her husband came home from work for lunch. Cybil greeted him with, "I have given a lot of thought to this situation with our son Neal. I have come to realize that I can no longer handle having him in the house overnight. It worries me when he picks on his sisters and slaps and punches them when he is high on drugs and liquor. I worry that he'll decide to cook himself a meal in the middle of the night and burn the house down.

"And I worry about you, that he is going to push you to the point of beating the daylights out of him when he comes around pickled to the gills on booze or gooned out on drugs. I don't want to see you in jail, honey. It scared the daylights out of me when he came over the other night acting like a wild man and you told me later you had started looking for your handgun as a way of dealing with him when he was out of control.

"The next time he asks to move back in, or even stay overnight, please respect my decision on this. He's welcome to visit, but not to stay."

Conner hugged his wife and said, "Okay, honey. I understand, and I'll back you up all the way."

The next evening Cybil and Conner had just come home from a movie when Neal rang the doorbell. Cybil greeted her son but noticed that his eyes were dilated and that he smelled strongly of liquor. They invited him in and visited for a few minutes. Cybil asked Neal if she could get him anything to eat or help him in any way. Each time he said, "No."

Cybil could no longer stand it and finally asked where he was staying that night.

He looked surprised and said, "Why, right here, in my room."

Cybil shook her head. "Neal, I discussed this situation with your dad yesterday and explained to him that I worry too much when you stay overnight in the house. Decide where you want to go, or we'll help you find a place."

Conner looked unhappy. "Cybil, we can't make him leave. One more night in the house isn't going to make that much difference."

Cybil was hurt but mustered her courage and said, "It would hurt me. If Neal is going to stay the night here, then I'm not. If that's the way it has to be, I'll get the girls and go to a motel.

"Neal, I love you and always will, but I can't stay in the same house overnight with you again. I'm always glad to have you visit, and I'd help you in any way possible. We all would, you know that!

"You get high to make yourself feel better. Now I'm going to have to do something to make *me* feel better when you are using, and high, or drunk, or all of the above."

(As you can see, there is a great deal of overlapping of the reactions to and types of behavior involved in alcoholism and addiction.)

What is the coaddict cycle? Why would anyone want to stay in what is basically a miserable situation?

People stay because at first not all of it is miserable. In fact, at first the rewards may be pretty good.

The coaddict cycle is very much like the addict cycle. It simply runs in the opposite direction:

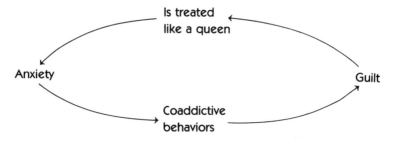

Case Study: Gary wonders how his parents' relationship ever got into the mess it is, with his mom an alcoholic and his dad close to a nervous breakdown because of it. He has no idea what things were like when they first began dating.

In those days, on Saturday nights, Sylvia's main interest was in "partying." She generally did this by calling a group of friends and making plans to go dancing. The partying always included a lot of drinking, and Sylvia always wanted her boyfriend, Gene, in on it.

Gene became a coaddict. When they went out together with her friends, Gene felt on top of the world. Sylvia would compliment him in front of other people, build him up, make him feel important. She let everyone know how great Gene was to be with and that no one could measure up to him as a man. Sylvia loved to dance in a way that got her a lot of attention, with moves that might have come off a floor show in Las Vegas. After a few drinks she and Gene usually put on a real show on the dance floor.

After a Saturday night out with Sylvia, Gene would think a lot about their evening together, about how other men had looked at her, and he would begin to worry. He concluded that if he couldn't be around Sylvia all the time, she might drop him and start seeing another man.

The next time they were out Gene was determined to stay with Sylvia all the time. She found him "hanging" on her the whole evening, even to the point of deciding when they would go to the restrooms. He became very short with the people around him, most of them her friends.

"Why don't you just relax?" Sylvia asked, a little short herself. "You aren't any fun when you are so uptight. Back off a little, you are embarrassing me!"

Gene began to feel bad that he wasn't trusting Sylvia. He answered, "Maybe you're right, Sylvia. I just find myself so jealous, and I know that all the men in the room would like to be with you." Sylvia responded by focusing on him totally, making him feel very special and important.

Gene's addiction to Sylvia merely grew with her addiction to alcohol.

How is the addict's cycle related to the coaddict's cycle?

The addict's cycle tends to fit hand in glove with the coaddict's cycle. The cycles reinforce each other in very subtle ways. The addict and coaddict keep each other sick. They need each other to maintain their addiction.

That is why you so often hear of someone divorcing an alcoholic and promptly marrying another alcoholic. It happens all the time.

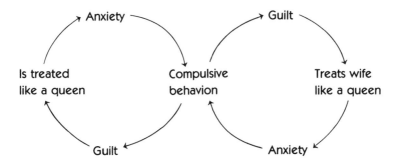

Case Study: Gregory was recently discharged from a chemical dependency center after successful treatment for addiction to cocaine. His wife, Annette, had participated in the treatment center's family program. Since his discharge, however, Annette had felt a growing sense of dissatisfaction.

Something was very different about Gregory now. He didn't mistreat her, but what she wanted was for him to treat her as he had in the past when he wasn't strung out on drugs.

At those times he was overcome with guilt and self-blame and would try to make up to her for whatever he had done in his last drug-using episode. Then Gregory had treated her like a queen. And Annette had thought that that was how he would behave to her all the time now that he wasn't using drugs.

The hitch was that now Gregory wasn't feeling guilty about anything, so he was just being himself.

Annette didn't quite know what to do. She finally realized that she had known Gregory the drug addict for so long that she didn't know Gregory the recovering addict at all. She also had no sense of what it should be like to be in a relationship with someone who wasn't using drugs.

All of this made Annette extremely uncomfortable and anxious. She began to wonder if Gregory were having an affair. To find out, she decided to follow him to and from work.

On the third day Gregory caught her, and she offered a not very believable excuse. "I was just bringing you your briefcase."

"Well, where is it, then?"

"Can you believe it? I followed you all the way downtown to bring the briefcase to you and I forgot to put it in the car."

Gregory stared at her. "Of course, you forgot to put it in the car because my briefcase is already in *my* car. Sometimes you drive me crazy, Annette. I think you were just following me."

Annette denied that. Later Gregory began to wonder if she were following him to make sure he actually was at work before she set out to meet a boyfriend.

The couple's three teenagers became caught up in the tangle of mistrust, suspicion, lack of communication, and misunderstood motives. Before long Gregory was back on drugs again.

Who is more obsessed, the addict or the coaddict?

While the addict is obsessed with using and the coaddict is obsessed with the addict's not using, both end up obsessed. The only difference is that the addict is addicted to a mood-altering substance or behavior, and the coaddict is addicted to the addict.

Sound complicated? It is—and isn't. The bottom line is that both persons will place their jobs, religion, finances, social lives, and children second to their individual addictions.

Case Study: Edna is the wife of Wayne, a successful businessman, who has a very expensive cocaine addiction. She hates his drug use and the types of people he deals with to get drugs.

She also hates dealing with creditors and making excuses when she must cover their inability to pay their bills. She hurts when she faces the children after she has had to sell something to make ends meet. She finds herself making excuses to her friends about missing furniture and possessions, when it is obvious that their expensive home is becoming more and more bare. She is beginning to find herself avoiding contact with many people outside of the family.

One day she confronted her husband. "Wayne, I want you to realize that we are about to lose this house. You don't get paid for two more weeks, and I don't see how we can make it until then. There isn't another thing I can sell or pawn. If you don't get off cocaine, we are all going down the tube."

Wayne hung his head and mumbled. He had been feeling terribly guilty about his drug use, what it was doing to their children, how it was affecting his life and threatening his career. A week earlier he had begun attending meetings of Narcotics Anonymous, although he didn't want to tell his wife; he had always refused to admit that he had a problem.

The next day he came home all smiles and handed her a roll of bills—enough to catch up on their payments and have some left over to get through the month. He also took her out to dinner at a nice restaurant.

Edna's feeling of relief was short-lived, however. She knew that the money couldn't have been from her husband's paycheck, and their savings were long gone. She had heard about addicts turning to crime, and she was paralyzed with fear that Wayne had robbed a store or something.

Wayne was too ashamed to tell her that he had bought cocaine for a friend while the man was out of work for a month, and the friend had just paid him back.

Soon Edna was searching Wayne's clothes and wallet, asking him pointed questions, obviously doubting the answers. And so the cycle began again . . .

How does the coaddict's behavior inadvertently keep the addictive cycle going?

The coaddict enables the addict to continue practicing his addiction, rather than the other way around, by protecting him from the consequences of his behavior. When he is drunk she calls his boss and says that he is sick. She turns down dinner invitations if she knows alcohol will be served. She makes excuses for his behavior.

When he drinks up his paycheck she pawns her jewelry and makes excuses to creditors.

In these and many other ways she acts as a buffer for the addict. In her attempts to "help" she insures that the addict will continue to drink or use.

Case Study: Laurel was very concerned about Terrance's drug use. She was afraid that he would lose his job. She was afraid that he couldn't pay the rent. She was afraid that her family would find out. She was afraid that *his* family would find out. She was afraid of what the kids would think.

In fact, she was afraid of everything.

In efforts to manage her own fear, her life became a frantic, nonstop effort to protect Terrance and herself from the consequences exposure might bring.

Terrance came home late one night, stoned. Even though his mother had called and said it was important, Laurel did not give him the message. She was afraid he would return the call at 2:30 a.m. and his mother would find out the condition he was in.

The next morning he was too sick to go to work; Laurel called in and said he had the flu. She hocked her wedding ring and some jewelry that had been her grandmother's to pay the rent.

Terrance never had to confront the problems his drug use was creating for them all because Laurel was so good at protecting him.

Six months later Terrance overdosed and was rushed to the hospital in a coma. He died a week later.

It was only then that Laurel began to see, dimly, that all her protecting of him might have been a big mistake, might have contributed to his death.

How does the coaddict trigger a relapse?

The coaddict and the addict tend to get locked into a game that could be called "Cops and Robbers." The coaddict is the "cop" who tries to police the addict's behavior. The addict tries to elude the coaddict's attempts at control. Round and round and round they go in a shatteringly destructive "dance/war."

If they are to stop this self-defeating game, they both have to change at the same time. All one-sided changes are destined to fail.

If the coaddict decides to trust the addict and if the addict continues to practice his addiction, he may sell her wedding ring for drugs. If the addict decides to quit using, the controlling behavior of the coaddict will convince him that he is untrustworthy and hopelessly guilty. He will then use to feel better about himself.

The situation often exists when the addict returns from treatment. He is no longer using. He is no longer practicing guilt-motivated behaviors such as "treating her like a queen."

What she wants is for him to be the way he was when he wasn't using but was feeling guilty. So she begins to stir up the guilt . . . "You never seem to care about me anymore," or "You spend as much time at work as you ever did at the bar."

That triggers his feelings of guilt. That in turn sets up his using again.

That is why it is *vital* for the coaddict to get treatment, too. Otherwise nothing is likely to change for the better permanently.

CHAPTER 7

"What Should I Tell My Friends?"

One of the many problems of children of addicted parents is the isolation that they feel. If one gets too close to other people, one might let slip— family secrets.

In these families, of course, a major part of the energy is invested in keeping secrets, not letting anyone know about Mom's little problem, Dad's little weakness. The parents may be pillars of the community, important business or professional people. Woe to the child who cracks the facade.

Case Study: The book *Bad Blood* by Richard M. Levine is the true story of a sixteen-year-old California girl, Marlene. She was the daughter of an alcoholic mother and a wimpy, indecisive father who protected his wife from the effects of her drinking and refused to make any effort to deal with it or the problems it was causing.

Family life had been a running battle between parents and daughter for years, and Marlene genuinely made attempts to get help. But when the family went for counseling or tried to deal with the problems with the law that Marlene's behavior was causing, and Marlene mentioned her mother's drinking, that invariably ended things and Marlene caught blazes for "washing our dirty linen in public."

Unable to stop the cycle or handle it, Marlene finally goaded her twenty-year-old boyfriend into murdering her mother and father.

Telling friends about your problems at home could have a number of consequences, from very positive to very negative. It is usually a matter of using your own best judgment.

It is possible that your friends already have an idea of what is wrong and for your sake haven't said anything. If they show that they know and are not going to judge you or cause problems, sometimes talking can bring a tremendous sense of relief. You might even find that friends have had similar problems in their lives.

But let's be honest. You could also lose friends because of your parents' problem.

Case Study: Jennifer and Mark had begun dating in their junior year in high school and liked each other a lot. They planned to go to the same university and even wanted to major in similar subjects. Mark felt a little humble that Jennifer dated him—she was one of the prettiest girls in school, as well as the daughter of a district judge and quite well off.

One afternoon, over snacks at a fast-food place, Jennifer asked casually about Mark's mother's moods. Mark had taken Jennifer to his house a few times, and his mother's mood swings had struck her as odd. About half the time she reacted as if Jennifer were a total stranger.

Mark did something very unusual—he told Jennifer that his mother was an alcoholic, that she was usually "knee-walking drunk" by noon, and that his family had managed to hide it from the world.

Jennifer was somewhat thrown by the information, but she didn't condemn Mark because of it. However, she telephoned him three days later in tears. She had told her little sister, and the little sister had passed it on to Dear Old Dad, who promptly forbade Jennifer to see Mark again.

"He said, 'What would people think?' and that you might turn out like that and a bunch of other nonsense," Jennifer wailed. "He wouldn't listen to a thing I said. He was really *awful* about it!"

Mark was devastated. His fear of turning out like his mother was so great that he had never so much as taken a sip of beer. Hearing this from Jennifer's stuffed shirt of a father was just too much.

Yet Jennifer's father's reaction is not uncommon. As many adult children of alcoholics can tell you, the stigma of being the son or daughter of "the town drunk" can last all your life.

Case Study: Caryn and Collette met when they were five and their families moved next door to each other. Although Caryn's family moved to another part of town when they were in the sixth grade, the girls remained best friends. Their birthdays were two weeks apart, and, because of the similarity in names, they joked that one birth certificate was in error and they were actually twins separated at birth.

Certainly they were as close as sisters, and in all the time they had known each other they had never had a serious disagreement.

The summer they turned sixteen Caryn pressed Collette to tell her what was wrong. She knew something was worrying her friend, and she felt sure it was something serious.

Somewhat reluctantly Collette did tell her. She had known for the past three or four years that her parents had been snorting cocaine now and then, on a "recreational" basis, she guessed they called it.

But about six months ago her father's company encountered some very serious business problems, and as his worries increased, so did his cocaine use. Now it was beginning to affect his behavior, the family finances, and his performance on the job. Collette was really frightened that her father might be becoming an addict.

Caryn was flabbergasted. She had no idea what to say. Her family was very religious, extremely strict in their beliefs. Caryn was not permitted to wear shorts in public, go to school dances, or attend other churches. She had once confided in Collette that she considered drug use "almost as bad a sin as murder."

Now she couldn't handle what Collette had told her. Over the next few weeks Collette saw her friend gradually pull away, ease out of the almost lifelong friendship.

"She was going places with other people, not returning my phone calls or making excuses not to talk to me, avoiding me at school."

The effect on Collette was devastating. "It was as if I weren't good enough for her anymore, as if what my parents did made *me* a less good person. I had been feeling not too great about myself before, but that just pushed me over the edge. By the end of that summer, between problems at home and being dumped by my best friend for something over which I had no control, I was thinking seriously of suicide. It was like losing a sister. I had no idea something could hurt that much."

Case Study: Alleta and Kerry were good friends, although neither considered the other a "best friend." So Alleta wasn't sure exactly why she invited Kerry to stop by her house one day and pick up a book she had promised to lend Kerry.

Although her parents were wealthy and considered among the town's leading "socialites," four or five times a week Alleta came home to find her mother passed out from drinking. On this particular day Mom was in her bedroom, and Alleta could tell from the snores that drifted down the stairs that she had been hitting the bottle again.

Alleta got the book and then abruptly blurted out to Kerry their "family problem" and the effect it was having on her father, older sister, and two little brothers.

Kerry stared at her. "Oh, man, do I know what you mean! *Exactly* what you mean," Kerry said, and then told Alleta about her alcohol- *and* drug-using father, who beat family members and more than once had had to be bailed out of jail for fights, drug possession, and once a robbery.

"Mom divorced him when I was twelve—I've never been so thankful for anything in my life. Mom started me going to Alateen when I was eleven, and that was what held me together and helped me get over Dad. I still go now and then. I'll go with you, if you want. It'll help, I promise."

It did help. Alleta found sympathy, understanding, freedom to express her feelings, and explanations of some of the things her mother did and the way they made her feel and react.

From being casual friends, Alleta and Kerry have

become very close, helping each other with a mutual problem that still now and then troubles their lives.

Telling your friends (if they don't already know) does have its risks, as shown by the case studies. It could improve your life or genuinely mar it. Use your own best judgment in the matter of whom you talk to.

But do go to Alateen. These meetings, for the children of alcoholics and addicts, will give you a chance to talk, to express what is going on in your life and how it is affecting you. Alateen will not help you to change a parent's behavior; as has been said before, that is difficult if not impossible for a child to do.

What Alateen does is help you to cope with your own feelings, your own reactions to your parents' problems.

It gives you friends who do understand, really understand.

As Lori, fifteen, put it, "I have to sneak around even to come to the meetings. When I once mentioned wanting to go my folks raised the roof. They said they didn't have a drinking problem and they weren't going to have everybody in town thinking that they did. They are both boozers and just won't admit it.

"But once I started going to the meetings I found out that even that wasn't unusual. A lot of kids at the meetings said their parents refused to admit that anything was wrong. They felt just the way I did about it.

"One of the big problems, living the way I did, was that you feel so cut off from other people. My folks didn't encourage me to have friends over, and I sure didn't push it. Who wants to bring in a friend when you might find your mother sitting on the couch in her underwear, whacked out of her mind?

"I knew my home life wasn't like most kids, and I didn't

feel like most kids. I felt—I don't know—marked by what my folks are like, and scarred by it in some way.

"But at Alateen I found that I wasn't alone, that there wasn't something wrong with me or my feelings. I found a lot of kids who felt just the same way. If my feelings were normal, maybe I wasn't a weirdo after all.

"I found friends who *understand*—I can't tell you how much that has meant to me."

CHAPTER 8

Family Roles

When one parent is chemically dependent and the other is a codependent, all of their children are affected by it, by the tremendous level of stress and pain that exists in addictive families.

Because of that, each child tends to act out a role in order to ease some of the pain, to make the family seem more normal, more like other families.

Typical family roles are the family hero, the scapegoat, the rebel, the distractor, the computer, the lost child, the mascot, the clown, the peacemaker, the switchboard, the martyr, the placator, the psychosomatic, the parentified child, the irrelevant one, the diplomat, and the warrior. Some of these roles overlap, and one child may sometimes play more than one role.

The Family Hero

The family hero is usually the eldest child. This child learns very early that he or she can relieve some of the pain of the family problem by getting members to focus on his or her successes.

The family hero may be a football player, a straight A

student, or captain of the debate team. It makes little difference as long as he or she is very successful. Often the family hero can be identified because he is all those things, and sometimes even more.

What the family hero doesn't get is to be a child.

Case Study: Betty Jo was an outstanding musician and also a great student. She managed to maintain a perfect 4.0 average, straight through grade school and high school. She was sophomore class president and a member of the student council.

She had a job after school, and on Saturdays she sang in the church choir. Everyone thought Betty Jo was wonderful, even her cocaine-addicted father.

Late one evening she arrived home from work and noticed that something seemed very wrong. Her mother had been crying, and her father seemed depressed. "What's wrong?" she asked, dreading the answer.

"I lost my job," her dad said, as her mother began to sob again.

Betty Jo rushed in with, "Let me tell you what happened at school today. Mrs. Kussic told me that I will be playing in the state finals. In fact, I'll be the only sophomore in the piano competition. Isn't that fantastic?"

Her mother mopped her eyes and said, "You're such a blessing, Betty Jo. I don't know what I would do without you."

Now her dad had tears in his eyes. "That goes double for me."

After everyone else was in bed, Betty Jo was still practicing. She was tired, and her wrists hurt. She was beginning to hate the piano, to feel as if it were a ball and chain around her ankle. But she just *had* to win that competition, for her family's sake.

The Family Scapegoat

A scapegoat is a child who takes all of the family pain upon himself or has it placed there by others. He or she underfunctions as badly as the family hero overfunctions. He seems incompetent in almost every part of his life. In fact, he is so incompetent that it is easy for others in the family to believe that almost everything wrong in the family is his fault.

Case Study: April's family was having a hard time paying their bills. There never seemed to be enough money to go around.

One day when April was twelve, her mother sent her to the store with a five-dollar bill to get a loaf of bread. "Now you be *sure* to get the right change, you hear?" her mother snapped.

April was instantly afraid. She knew they would give her the wrong change! All the way to the store she worried about it. How much was bread, anyway? she wondered. At the store she picked out a loaf of bread that, with tax, would cost exactly one dollar. She knew that she would get four dollars back. This was going to be easy.

The clerk rang up her purchase and gave her exactly four dollars back. She was thrilled. Mom would be proud of her this time, she thought. Holding the bread in one hand and the four bills in the other, she started home at a run. But about a block from the house she tripped and fell, and the money went flying.

She managed to round all of it up, but then she noticed the bread. It was lying in the street, and a car had run over it.

Sadly she returned to the store and bought another loaf of bread.

When April got home, head hanging, shoulders slumped, her mother took one look at her and said, "You got the wrong change, didn't you? I *knew* you would!"

April said, "Yes, Mom. I'm sorry . . ."

"Sorry doesn't make up for anything! Sorry doesn't make the house payment! And people wonder why we can't pay our bills, why money is so short around here . . ."

Nobody mentioned that Dad's cocaine habit cost them $150 a day.

The Family Rebel

The person who functions as the family rebel takes a basically defiant stance with the family and with almost everyone else. He or she is saying, "You'll never control me!"

The rebel actually believes that he or she is not like others in the family. He fails to realize that the very act of rebelling makes him very much a part of the family. The rebel often gets so much attention that other family members do not notice their own pain.

Case Study: Amy was fourteen and angry at the world in general and her drug-addicted parents in particular. She had ditched school thirty-two times this year and had been suspended three times. Even when she was in school, she paid little attention to the teachers and rarely, if ever, handed in her homework.

One day, after a particularly painful chewing-out by the principal, Amy decided that she really would try to do better. Besides, there was a new guy in school, Sam, who she thought was the cutest guy she'd ever seen. But he was a straight A student and she had seen his disgusted look when the teacher asked for her homework and she said, "I don't have it."

That afternoon she started on her assignments right after school. Then her father came home, stoned to the eyebrows on speed. He was moving through the house nonstop, talking like a one-man filibuster, with her mother following him shrieking, "Where's mine? Did you shoot mine, too?"

The cursing and verbal abuse began, followed by the fighting. She hated that and did what she so often did when it started: took some clothes and went to stay at a girlfriend's house. At school the next day the teacher rolled his eyes and said, sarcastically, "Oh, sure," when she tried to explain that she had forgotten her homework. And Sam looked disgusted again. After class he looked away when she smiled and said "Hi" to him.

At noon she was caught having sex with Billy in his car in the school parking lot. In her purse was an expensive watch, shoplifted that morning from a store near the school. She and Billy were expelled, and now she is in trouble with the law as well.

The Family Distractor

The distractor is a person who always changes the subject when anything serious or potentially painful or threatening comes up. He or she runs away, emotionally, from everything.

Case Study: Darla had tried to talk to her father about this before. She wanted to know his version of why her parents had gotten a divorce and whether his drinking had had anything to do with it. This time she thought she had the perfect opportunity. Her stepmother had gone to town to buy groceries, and she was alone on the farm with her father.

She said, "Dad, why did you and Mom split up? I'd really like to know."

He seemed to be thinking it over, and Darla felt hopeful. Maybe she would finally hear his side of the story. Then he said, "Come on outside. I want to show you something."

They walked to the chicken yard, and her father said, "You see that rooster? I got that rooster for fifty cents and I paid two dollars for a couple of hens and now look, I've got about twenty chickens. I'll bet you always wondered how I got a yard full of chickens and it only cost me two dollars and fifty cents."

Darla, who had never wondered anything of the sort, now said so and added, "But, Dad, what I have wondered about was . . ."

"Come over here and let me show you the new calf I got last week." Darla got the Cook's tour of the pigs, the ducks, the horses, the farm machinery, but she never found out about the divorce and what caused it.

Pinning down a distractor is like trying to nail jelly to a wall. Darla's father was a distractor.

The Family Computer

The computer only thinks, never feels. He or she deals with pain by not feeling it. Such a person intellectualizes everything, seeing it only, thinking about it only, but never feeling it.

Case Study: Shawn's grandmother had just passed away, and the minister had come to their home to see how everyone was getting along. He was particularly interested in how Shawn was doing, because Shawn's mother had said that he never shed a tear when the phone call came from the hospital saying she had died. Shawn was close to his grandmother—the minister did not know that it was because of both parents' frequent drug use.

Pastor Johnson said, "Shawn, how do you feel about your grandmother's death?"

Shawn shrugged. "It was time. She was in her 70 s, and her health hadn't been good."

"I know all that, but how do you feel?"

"Well, everybody has to go sooner or later."

"Shawn," the pastor said, "those are thoughts. I want to know how you *feel* about it now."

"I feel like it was her time."

"That still isn't a feeling, Shawn. Don't you have feelings about it?"

No matter how hard he tried, the pastor could not get Shawn to talk about his feelings. Shawn was like a computer. All he could give was the facts.

The Lost Child

The lost child is the kid who just doesn't matter. He or she is left out of everything. He is withdrawn and often seems depressed.

This is the kid who never gets noticed. He could be in a group with four other kids and few of them would even speak to him. He seems to fade into the background.

Case Study: Jill was sitting at the lunch counter with her friends. The waiter took orders from them but didn't seem to notice Jill. Some of her friends finished eating and left.

Jill was hungry, but she never said a thing. It was that way at home, too. If her alcoholic father didn't notice her, he was less likely to hit her. She was not aware of how much that role at home was making her The Invisible Girl in public and at school.

Now she began to worry that someone would notice that she hadn't been waited on. That would be embarrassing. Finally a waitress said, "Oh, I thought you were with them," indicating a couple just leaving. Jill didn't reply.

"Did you want anything?" the waitress asked.

Jill shook her head. "No, I was just resting a minute," she said and got up and hurried out.

The Family Mascot

Mascots are peculiar people. They manage to be cute all the time. They are cute, cute, cute, even though they may not be pretty.

Mascots never grow up. They can still seem to be six years old when they get to be forty. Anytime they are in the room, all eyes are on them. They don't seem to do anything a lot of the time, but they always attract attention. They are, in many ways, amazing people.

Case Study: Kim came home from school one day to find her mother with a living room full of women for a meeting of her Garden Club.

Kim's mother was also a heroin addict, and now she was on the verge of "nodding off." Kim had great "radar." She seemed to sense when Mom was about to embarrass herself. Now she walked into the room and, as usual, everyone looked at her.

She turned up the radio and said, "Let me show you this new dance. I bet you'll *love* it!" She began dancing to the music, then volunteered to teach the women the dance.

Two hours later Kim, lively and vivacious and "cute," was still showing the women dances. No one noticed that her mother was now sound asleep and drooling.

The Family Clown

Family clowns perform the same function as did the well-known "gallows humor." In a certain town in Europe they hanged criminals on Sunday afternoons, and most of the townspeople turned out for the occasion. As each criminal approached the gallows, he stopped and told the funniest joke he knew. Everyone laughed uproariously. Then the noose was placed around the criminal's neck and he was executed.

It was said that the people laughed so as not to cry. That is the function of the family clown.

Case Study: Jerry was watching as his father washed the car. The next-door neighbor was standing talking with Dad. Jerry's older brother drove up just as his mother came out the front door. Jerry saw that she was staggering as she started down the stairs.

Immediately Jerry jumped to his feet, pointed to his brother, and shouted, "Good grief! Kill it before it multiples! Dad, anyone has a right to be ugly, but that guy is abusing the privilege. You've heard of whipped with an ugly stick? He wasn't—the whole *tree* fell on him. Tell me, Dad, did you have any kids besides me that lived?"

By now everyone was laughing, and no one noticed that Mom was drunk—again.

The Family Peacemaker

A family peacemaker makes peace at all costs. This is the person in the family whose self-appointed mission it is to stop family conflict.

While that has its good points, the problem with having a peacemaker in the family is that other members are never able to work through their disagreements and settle them.

Case Study: Cami always became very anxious when people in her family were angry with each other, because it usually made even worse her alcoholic father's rages and verbal abuse of them all.

Her little brother, Kyle, had gotten into their father's coin collection and used the coins to play Monopoly. Several of them had been lost. Dad had been furious with Kyle and wound up yelling at everybody.

So Cami set out to make things right. She got a list of the missing coins and at coin shops was able to replace most of them. The only trouble was that to do so she had to sell a ring that had been her grandmother's.

When she gave the coins to her father he was very happy —until he heard about the ring. Then he blew up again.

Now Cami didn't know what to do. She didn't want her father angry at her either. To make matters worse, Kyle had gotten into the collection again and lost more coins.

This time Cami took money out of her savings for college to replace the additional lost coins and buy back her grandmother's ring.

While Cami's efforts to keep peace were understandable, she needed to let Kyle learn to stay out of things he was not supposed to be into and to find the coins he had lost.

The Family Switchboard

The family switchboard is the member who behaves like a telephone switchboard. All significant communication goes through this person, especially when there is a possibility of conflict between family members.

Case Study: Lucy's father noticed that his wife seemed awfully quiet. He began to worry that she might be angry with him. The longer she remained quiet, the more he worried. Finally, when he could stand it no longer, he went upstairs to Lucy's room and knocked on the door. Lucy told him to come in.

"I'm worried that your mother is mad at me about something," he said. "I was wondering if you would be willing to talk to her and find out if she's angry and if so, about what."

Neither one said that Mom's being angry often sent her into an alcoholic binge. They both knew that.

"Okay, Dad, I'll find out." She went downstairs and sat on the couch next to her mother. "Mom, Dad's been wondering if you're mad at him about something. Are you?"

"I certainly am!" Mom said sharply. "Yesterday I found a matchbook in his coat pocket. It had 'Doris, 729-5552, husband out of town on Wednesdays' written on it in his handwriting. Don't you think I have a reason to be upset with him?"

"Well . . . maybe. Let's see what he has to say about it." She went back upstairs and relayed the message to her father.

He burst out laughing and said, "Well, I can certainly see where she's coming from, but she's mistaken as to the meaning of what she read. I was at lunch with a customer two days ago when my pager went off and my secretary told me to call Doris, a longtime customer of ours. When I called her, she said could I demonstrate our product line to her and her husband—on any day but Wednesday, because he is out of town on Wednesdays."

Lucy really laughed at that, then went down and told her mother the truth about the message in the matchbook.

Her mother laughed, too. Then Lucy went and told her father that everything was fine. Dad went downstairs and began watching television with his wife.

The Family Martyr

The family martyr is the member who relieves the stress on the family system by appearing to sacrifice herself or himself. The martyr always sacrifices just in time to keep anyone from noticing that something is very wrong in the rest of the family.

Case Study: Kent's parents' drug use kept the family constantly broke, so it was no surprise to Kent to find his little sister Ginnie in tears one Saturday evening. Her best friend's birthday party was that night, and her mother had just told her there was no money for Ginnie to buy a present. Moreover, Kent realized, she probably couldn't go to the party anyway. Neither parent was in any condition to drive.

Kent had been looking forward to this evening. He had a date with a girl he'd had a crush on for a long time, and he planned to take her someplace special. But if Ginnie didn't take a present or even go to the party . . .

"Mop up, kid," Kent said from between clenched teeth. "I'll give you the money for a present and take you to the party," and he went to telephone the girl to tell her he wouldn't be able to make it.

That sort of thing had happened before, more than once. Kent knows it is his parents' fault, yet increasingly he resents Ginnie and his other sister, Lois.

The Family Placator

The family placator is the member who relieves stress in the family system by convincing other members that everything is just fine. This is the person who works hard to make everyone else in the family think things are really okay, no matter how many troubles and problems there are.

Case Study: Kristen was extremely upset. She knew that her father had drunk up a sizeable portion of his paycheck while her mother was visiting her sister in California. To make matters worse, her mother's plane was due at 8:30 p.m. and Dad hadn't come home from work yet.

So she took her mother's car and went to the airport. When her mother had retrieved her luggage and placed it in the car, Kristen said casually, "Dad has really been having a bad time of it lately. He has missed you so much. He's said several times that he couldn't sleep alone in that king-sized bed, so I told him what he needed was a night out with the boys. It was the only thing I could think of that might help. After all, it was you he really wanted to be with, and you were gone."

It was a thin story and Kristen knew it: If Dad had really wanted to be with Mom he'd have met her at the airport. But Mom appeared to buy it, and Kristen breathed a little easier. Maybe that would keep the lid on things for a while.

The Psychosomatic

The psychosomatic family member is the person who relieves stress in the family by being "sick." This person often has stress-induced ulcers, migraine headaches, skin rashes, or asthma. He or she may be anorexic or have revolving-door diabetes—diabetes that should be medically controlled but isn't; he responds to family problems by going into acidosis, indicating that the prescribed amount of insulin is no longer sufficient to control the diabetes.

That is not "faking it"—pretending to be ill. The problems are genuine, and the person's state of health is usually an indication of what things are like at home.

Case Study: Naomi's parents, both half drunk, were fighting again. She hated that, but it happened a lot. All the time, in fact.

Now her father was yelling, "If you don't shut up I am going to divorce you! I've had all of this I'm going to put up with!"

"Divorce, divorce, divorce!" her mother screeched. "All I ever hear from you is divorce! Every time things get a little tough, you want to run away. That's the story of your life! Your're just like your father—a real coward! If you had been in the army instead of running away to Canada, they would have court-martialed you for cowardice!"

Naomi could feel her chest tightening, and she began to wheeze. Her father was shouting, "If you were any good as a wife, I wouldn't be thinking about divorce all the time!"

Naomi was struggling to breathe. She went into the kitchen where her parents were, wheezing and unable to talk. Then she fainted. Her parents forgot their fight and rushed to her rescue.

Parentified Child

A parentified child reduces family stress by taking over one or both of the parents' roles. This typically happens in families where one or both parents behave incompetently in response to stress.

Case Study: Harvey's father came home drunk one evening. He stood in the living room slurring his words and weaving as he tried to talk to his son. Harvey was painfully aware that his mother was in the kitchen cooking dinner and would be deeply hurt if she realized that her husband was drunk again after his promises to quit.

So Harvey talked his father into going upstairs to bed.

He never mentioned that his father was home until his mother began to worry about him and wonder if he might have been in an accident.

Two days later Harvey came home to find his father passed out on the living room floor. He managed to carry him upstairs, undress him, and put him to bed.

Three weeks later Harvey got a telephone call at school. His father was in jail for being drunk and disorderly. His mother was out of town—would Harvey come and get him?

He did.

A week later his father was arrested for driving under the influence. This time Harvey couldn't get him out of jail because the bail was too high. So he called his grandmother and explained the situation. His grandmother gave him the money, and Harvey got his father out.

"I don't feel like Dad's son," Harvey once told a friend. "I feel like his baby-sitter." That, really, is the role Harvey has taken on.

The Irrelevant One

The irrelevant one is a family member who relieves the stress in the family system by raising extraneous, unimportant issues. He does this during any time of great pain in the family.

Case Study: Jordan's father and his uncle, both drinking, were having another of their "family disagreements." Jordan often wondered if these were "disagreements," what would fights be like? They seemed typical of his father's side of the family.

Now Uncle George was yelling, "We should have used the nuclear bomb in Vietnam. That would have put an end to the war."

"You jerk!" his father bellowed. "If we had used a nuclear bomb, they would have used a nuclear bomb."

"Are you kidding?" Uncle George's voice rose a notch. "The North Vietnamese didn't have nuclear bombs."

"Hey, Jordan," his father yelled, "come over here. Tell this idiot you've got for an uncle that the Vietnamese had nuclear bombs."

Jordan said, "I just heard that the Iranians are trying to make a nuclear bomb. Besides that, what would they do with the nuclear waste? It's a very small country."

"Are you talking about Vietnam or Iran?" asked his father.

"Panama is a small country, too."

The Family Diplomat

The family diplomat deals with stress by negotiating settlements among two or more family members. While that sounds like a positive thing to do in a family system, if it becomes a way of life it prevents other members from learning to resolve their own conflicts.

Case Study: Mollie's parents were having trouble deciding where the family should go on vacation. Mom wanted to go to the mountains because she liked to camp and hike. Dad wanted to go to the ocean; he liked to lie on the beach, surf, and ·swim. Mollie didn't know why they argued about it—both of them spent most of the time drinking anyway.

But last year the battle had dragged on until summer was over and they hadn't had a vacation at all.

Now, as her parents' voices began to rise, Mollie hurried between them and said brightly, "Mom and Dad, I've got it! We could go to California. That way we would be within twenty minutes of the mountains *and* the beach. We could take turns going to the mountains, then to the ocean."

That worked—they agreed to go to California, although Mollie knew that they would soon be fighting about something else. Like most children of addicts or alcoholics, Mollie often feels as if *she* is the one raising two children.

The Family Warrior

The family warrior takes the stress off the family system by creating a conflict with a nonfamily member. If a suitable nonfamily member is not available, the family warrior sometimes starts a less intense conflict with a family member. That diverts everyone's attention to a less vital conflict.

Case Study: Owen was very afraid. He knew that his father had sold some of his mother's jewelry, including an antique brooch. His mother loved her antique jewelry, and the brooch had been her favorite, given to her by a great-aunt.

His mother said, "Owen, have you seen my brooch?"

"No, Mom."

She looked at her husband and asked, "Tom, do you know where my . . . " Her voice trailed away at the expression on his face. "Oh, no! Tom, how could you?"

"But baby, you know we had to pay the rent."

Owen's mother opened her mouth, probably to say that his father's cocaine habit had something to do with not having the rent money. But before she could speak Owen jumped up and shouted at his brother, "Damn you, you pig! You took the last pork chop. You always take the last of everything—you never care about anyone but yourself!" With that Owen threw milk in his brother's face. Soon the two of them were slugging it out. Owen's parents were forced to separate the boys.

When it was over, they were sent to their rooms. The brooch was never mentioned again.

If an addicted family had enough children, it might be possible for each child to play one of these roles. In most families, however, children may act out any number of roles, depending on the kinds of stress the family is experiencing.

The important thing to remember is that a child who plays any of these roles is behaving in an unhealthy way.

Most people will identify the family rebel as a child needing help, but very few people recognize that the family hero is also in need of help.

CHAPTER 9

You and Your Brothers and Sisters

There is another role you may have to play, especially if you are the oldest in the family. That role is "parent" to younger brothers and sisters, particularly if your parents are not functioning in their roles.

You may be the one who has to impose rules on younger kids or take them places, see that they keep their dentist appointments, keep them from pigging to the eyebrows on junk food, break up fights.

Much of the time that is not a particularly rewarding experience. The younger kids resent you and are likely to say, "You aren't my boss!"

It may be tempting sometimes to be too hard on them— maybe you can't control your parents, but by gosh you *can* control the state of your little brother's room or what little sister spends her allowance on. The kids are right when they say you are being a tyrant.

You may also take it hard when they have problems. It can seem like your fault that your little brother got into a fight in school and is now in the principal's office.

Your parents can react in a number of ways to your

trying to take over their job. They may resent it. They may see themselves as being perfectly capable of handling it. They may happily push the role off on you—it gets them out from under the responsibility. Or they may not even be aware that you are trying in some ways to fill their shoes.

Sometimes they have all those reactions, which confuses everybody.

If you are acting as the parent, realize that you can't really take over the role and that there are limits to what you can do. You are, after all, basically still a kid.

Be reasonable with young brothers and sisters. Exercising authority just to exercise authority is never a good decision, even if it makes you feel good right then. It's too easy to slip into being an obnoxious jerk and breed resentment in them.

Try to be consistent. Uncertainty is already a big factor in everyone's life. Don't add to it if you can help it.

If you are a younger member of the family and an older brother or sister is trying to act as Mom or Dad or both, try not to make things harder. Your brother or sister has taken on a difficult role (or had it pushed off on him or her) and may not enjoy it one whit more than you enjoy having him or her telling you what to do.

Try to cooperate with each other and get along as well as you can. You are trying to cope with a very difficult situation. Conflict between yourselves will just make it worse.

Case Study: Kinley is sixteen, Matthew is twelve, and Raven is nine. Their parents are divorced; their mother is an alcoholic. Her first act when she comes home from work is to reach for a bottle. She has usually passed out by 8 o'clock.

Kinley is the one who makes Matt and Raven do their

homework and sees that they have clothes ready for schoo. the next day.

Now and then Mom comes out of her alcoholic stupor and becomes "Supermom." She cleans the house to a shine, waxes floors, bakes cookies, takes the kids to the park or the zoo on weekends. And she sometimes shows her resentment at Kinley's taking over her role. Unfortunately, those times don't last. Before long she is drinking again.

Matt and Raven also resent Kinley's acting as Mom. In fact, Kinley feels, Matt sometimes goes out of his way to be obnoxious. One day when Matt had flatly refused to clean his room (Kinley had walked in and said, "Were there any survivors of whatever happened here?"), he and Kinley wound up in a shouting match, with Raven joining in that she was *not* going to do her homework tonight.

"You're not my boss!" Raven howled.

"All right," Kinley said quietly, "You don't like my trying to hold things together around here. I've been thinking for quite a while about going to live with Dad. You want to be on your own—maybe that would be better for everyone."

Once Matt and Raven had a chance to think it over, they realized that it wouldn't be better. Kinley cooked most of their meals, saw that they had something to wear to school that looked good, made sure they had lunch money— things Mom couldn't be trusted to do.

The three sat down and talked out some of their differences. Kinley realized that she had been harder on them than was probably necessary, and she agreed to ease up on some of the rules and regulations.

All three agreed that they had enough to cope with handling Mom's problem without being at each other's throats as well.

CHAPTER 10

How Your Parents' Addiction Affects You

T eenagers who grow up in a home where one or both parents are addicted to drugs or alcohol often think that they are the only ones who feel the way they do. That is not true.

All children of addicted parents have the following problems:

1. They tend to isolate themselves, and they are frightened of authority figures.

Gary had always felt guilty about his dad's drinking. In fact, he sometimes thought he was responsible for it. He tried over and over to get better grades, to make Dad proud, not to anger him. But nothing he did made any difference.

Gary also had a terrific crush on Eileen, although he never got up the nerve even to speak to her. One day when he came home he found Eileen helping his mother as part of a "Maid for a Club" school project. When he walked in, Eileen was in the kitchen ironing shirts. Mom winked at him—she knew how he felt about Eileen. When Eileen had finished her chores Mom said, "Honey, why don't you drive Eileen home?"

Gary's heart jumped. He would finally get a real chance to talk to Eileen.

There was only one problem: Dad had the keys to the car, and he was in the den drunk as usual. When Gary asked for the keys, Dad bellowed, "What the #¢$% do you want the @#¢$%@ keys for, anyway?"

Gary cringed and said in a small voice, "To take Eileen home."

Dad fished in his pocket for the keys and tossed them to Gary, saying, "Just don't get her pregnant!"

Gary died a thousand deaths as he took the keys. He glanced at Eileen—her face was fiery red. Not a word was exchanged between Gary and Eileen as they drove. Gary knew he would never have the nerve to speak to her again. He would also be sure that nobody invited kids to his house again.

2. They tend to be approval seekers and have little sense of their own identity.

Children of alcoholics want desperately to be accepted, something they may never have received at home.

Linda and her sister Joanne saved their money for a pumpkin for Halloween. When they got it home, they asked Mom to carve it for them. The only problem was that Mom was "that way" again.

She cut the top off the pumpkin, then scooped out handfuls of the insides and threw them violently on the floor, screaming, "You wanted this damned pumpkin, you clean up the mess."

Because they were afraid of Mom's anger, they did as they were told. They even acted happy that Mom was "letting" them help. Later, when Mom slipped cutting the mouth and ruined the pumpkin, they acted as if it didn't matter.

Children of addicts lose any sense of who they are and what they feel. They seek approval from others, never realizing that something very precious is being sacrificed: their own sense of identity.

3. They are frightened by anger and criticism.

Keith Jr. was so proud of himself. He had bought his father an ice cream cone. Not just any ice cream cone, but Big Keith's favorite, Rocky Road. And not only Rocky Road, but a double scoop!

He imagined how happy Keith would be. But when he actually handed the ice cream to Big Keith, not a word was spoken. Big Keith started to eat it, but his hands were unsteady and the top scoop fell off and landed in his lap. He started to swear furiously and yelled, "What is wrong with you? You know I hate sticky stuff on me! Can't you do anything right?" Then Big Keith began to hit him.

Children of alcoholics or addicts never know when criticism and anger will lead to abuse—emotional, physical, sexual, or all three.

4. They feel guilty when they stand up for themselves.

These teenagers truly believe that they are unworthy. They think that they have no right to say who they are. Emotional abuse has always been a part of their lives.

Debbie's alcoholic mother created a world of rules—you must do this, you must always wear the perfect outfit, you must never say anything like that—and any time Debbie inadvertently broke a rule her mother was furious. Debbie's acceptance was always based on performance. Over and over she had heard, "You're nothing but trash. You'll never amount to anything."

One day the home ec teacher came in and found everyone in Debbie's kitchen throwing muffins at each other. All except Debbie, who was standing quietly to one side. The teacher slapped a detention slip on everyone, until Debbie said, "But I didn't do anything," and the others agreed that she hadn't.

Later Debbie felt terribly guilty, as if she should have been in detention, too. In fact, she waited after school until her friends got out of detention and walked home with them.

5. They develop either under- or overresponsibility.

Kids who have been blamed for everything in an addicted parent's life either become addicted to trying to "fix" everything, or they become helpless.

Cindy opened the bathroom door to find her father mainlining heroin, holding a needle, a cord tied around his arm. He screamed at her, "What do you expect? You and that mother of yours! I wouldn't need to do this if it weren't for you!"

After that Cindy felt as if it was her fault every time Dad didn't come home. She felt responsible when her little sisters were hungry or she heard Mom crying late at night. She found herself doing things like collecting and selling empty pop bottles so her sisters could eat. When Dad was really wiped out, she hid his car keys so he couldn't drive. In fact, she seemed more like a parent than he did.

Billy responded differently to the stress in his family. He also believed that his dad's drug use was his fault, but he had given up long ago.

Dad constantly said things like, "You screw up everything you touch. You're accident-prone. Oh, God, don't let Billy fix it."

When Billy's little sister was hungry, Billy cried. When Dad came home angry, Billy hid until Dad was asleep.

Children of drug-abusing parents tend to grow up too quickly or too slowly. They have to behave like adults or like infants.

6. Children of addicts tend to look for "victims" to help.

These kids often identify with the underdog, because they are victims, too. They have been robbed of their childhood. They feel sorry for others because it would be too painful to feel sorry for themselves.

Janice liked to pick up and find homes for stray dogs because she was sure they would get run over if she didn't help them.

She also wanted to help little Jamie who lived in the apartment below her. The other kids seemed to pick on Jamie.

One day several of them were making fun of Jamie. Janice stepped in and told them to leave Jamie alone. One of the kids grabbed Janice's earring and ripped it off, cutting her ear.

The next day Jamie told Janice to leave her alone.

That evening Dad noticed that Janice was upset. He began to ridicule her, saying, "Oh, look at the crybaby! Aren't you a little old for that?"

No one ever helped Janice.

7. They become addicted to excitement (chaos).

Adolescents growing up in severely disturbed homes live in a cycle. Graphically, it looks like this:

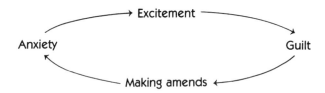

Excitement takes many forms in the family with an addicted parent. A child never knows when a parent will come home, whether the parent will be straight or loaded, kind or abusive, whether the utilities will be on or off. The child feels depressed a good deal of the time. But when a crisis occurs the family all draws together. Dad may even take charge, and everybody does his part to overcome the problem.

Larry came home to find yet another electricity cutoff notice on the door. He could feel his heart pounding as he rushed into the house and to the telephone. Mom really sounded concerned and was home in minutes. She took charge, sending Larry to Uncle John's store for a loan. Roy went to Aunt Phyllis' house, and Rick called Dad, getting him only after an argument with their stepmother. But everyone helped and by evening the electricity was on again. As the utility truck pulled away, Mom said, "Larry, if you didn't leave the lights on all day, I could pay this bill myself."

All of the adults looked at Larry. He felt terrible—it was

all his fault. The next morning he got up early, cooked breakfast for his brothers and his Mom, and washed the dishes. When he got home from school, he cooked dinner and tried to get his homework done.

Trying to get the potatoes done at the same time as the peas was hard. Trying to concentrate on his homework while trying to get the peas and potatoes done made him very nervous.

And Mom didn't come home that night.

Was she just drunk, or had she been in an accident? Wondering and worrying about it, Larry stayed awake until after midnight. Mom still wasn't home when they went to school the next morning. Larry couldn't even think that day.

That night she came home right after work as though nothing had happened. Nobody mentioned her not being home the night before.

When Larry got home from school the next day there was a letter from the landlord: "Your rent is past due. If not paid immediately, you will have to vacate your apartment." Larry ran for the telephone. His heart was beating wildly.

Children growing up with an addicted parent become addicted to a chaotic style of life. They begin to see it as normal. They live from crisis to crisis. The only time they feel good about themselves is during a crisis.

8. They confuse love with pity.

These children have never experienced real love. They grow up never having had a chance to give love to others or feel love for themselves. They have learned to feel sorry for themselves, but not to love themselves.

Phillip's parents were both alcoholic. He was uncertain what to do around them most of the time. They fought constantly, calling each other horrible names. When his mother really got onto Dad, Phillip had "warm feelings" for him. He thought that was love.

If his mother said enough hateful things, his father would explode and beat her viciously. Afterward Phillip would wipe the blood from her face, all the while crying and saying, "I love you, Mom," over and over.

Phillip felt sorry for his mother, but he didn't love her. He had never known what love was because no one had ever loved him. Addicted people always put their addiction before other people.

When Phillip began dating, he found someone he could feel sorry for. Betty Lou's mother was terribly abusive to her. There had been times when she tied Betty Jo to a post in the basement and beat her unconscious. Phillip often held Betty Lou for hours, telling her of his love and saying that he would marry her and take her away to a safe place.

9. They tend to deny feelings.

Children who grow up in homes where one of the parents is addicted tend to distance themselves from their feelings. They have learned to protect themselves by denying what they feel.

Greg was feeling closer all the time to his new stepbrother. This was the first time they had gone to the movies together. Now Greg tried to give John a hug. He had always given Dad a hug. But now he felt his stepbrother stiffen and pull away.

John said, "What are you, some kind of queer or something?"

Greg didn't know what a queer was, but he knew it wasn't good. He felt hurt, and tears came to his eyes.

John said, "What's wrong with you now? You're just a big sissy."

Greg couldn't know that living with an alcoholic father most of his life had made John the way he was, that feelings were unacceptable to him, that to acknowledge feelings opened him up to ridicule.

10. They judge themselves harshly and have low self-esteem.

Charley had wanted to be a writer all her life, something that her drug-using parents found hilarious. One day at school the teacher announced an essay contest for tenth-graders. The first prize was $500, which to Charley sounded like a fortune.

She wrote her essay and rewrote it, but as the deadline approached she began to feel more and more that it was "just a lot of silly kid stuff." She didn't bother to send it in.

Two days later the English teacher stopped her after class and handed her her essay; it had been turned in accidentally with a homework assignment.

"Charley, why on earth didn't you submit this? It is excellent."

Charley just shuffled her feet and mumbled, "I thought it was too dumb. My folks say the stuff I write is usually dumb."

"Charley, I was one of the judges in that contest. This is much better than the paper that won."

11. They overcompensate by acting superior.

Acting superior is one of the primary defenses against the pain of living in an alcoholic family.

Peter knew that his father wouldn't be coming home that night. After all, it was payday. It didn't matter that Peter's jeans had holes in them and were too short now. By the time Dad got home all the money would be gone.

Peter liked Roberta, but that morning he had seen her looking at his ankles, all too visible now. But that evening Roberta walked up to him and handed him an envelope. He opened it and read, "Roberta Thomas requests your presence at a birthday party given in her honor . . ." He didn't read the rest of it. He knew he couldn't go to a party in his scruffy clothes, and he didn't have money for a present.

He sniffed and said, "I don't go to seventh-graders' stupid parties. They're so immature." Roberta's smile faded as Peter turned away and shouted, "Hey, Jack, look what this dumb chick handed me. Can you believe it?"

The two boys took off together, laughing. No one noticed how depressed Peter was for the next several weeks.

Children growing up in drug-abusing homes learn only a few coping mechanisms. Their parents are not the best role models from whom to learn healthy coping strategies. Acting superior may be perceived as less painful than the other alternative: accepting the fact that their whole lives are painful.

12. They are dependent and terrified of being abandoned.

Children with drug-abusing parents have no opportunity to experiment with independence before it is thrust upon them. Consequently, they never really achieve it.

One of the first things Carlos can remember is waking up in his father's car with his little brother, Juan, crying. It was cold, and he was hungry. He rubbed the sleep from his eyes and looked around.

There were a few other cars and a building with lights not far away. He could hear music and laughter coming from the building.

Then the door opened, and a man came out. He stumbled against the car, then saw Carlos and began to scream at him and beat his fists on the car window.

Carlos was terrified. The man continued to scream and beat on the window for a long time before he finally left. It was much longer before Carlos' father returned.

Carlos is seventeen now, and he still hates being alone. He sees himself as a helpless victim most of the time. His girlfriend, Julia, often leaves him to dance with other boys at the club where they hang out, and Carlos hates that. Once she left with Phil and didn't return for over an hour. A friend told Carlos that he had seen them making out in Phil's car. Furious, Carlos drove home alone. But in a couple of hours Julia called. She said she was sorry, would he come back to the club?

He would. He was on his way in minutes.

Julia has done this to him more than once, and he has always taken her back. Each time his self-image is a little lower and he behaves more dependently. Carlos is terrified that one day Julia won't come back.

13. They do not know what "normal" is.

These children grow up in homes that are not normal. The way their parents relate to each other and to them is not normal. Behavior in their families is not normal. In fact, very little of their experience in life is normal.

Janette saw her stepfather's behavior as normal. It was how she had grown up. Every morning he would break two raw eggs in a large glass and fill the glass with whiskey. Janette thought that was normal.

She also thought that all her friends' fathers had sex with them—until one day she asked her best friend, Mitzi. Mitzi acted shocked and disgusted, and Janette felt that she had made a horrible mistake by asking. She felt betrayed by Mitzi. After all, they had talked about everything else. Now Mitzi acted as if this was a big deal. Well, it wasn't to Janette. After all, her stepfather had sex with both of her older sisters, and besides Mom was often so tired.

Maybe Mitzi just didn't want her as a friend any longer. Janette began screaming at Mitzi because she was such a traitor.

Children of drug-abusing parents have not had life experiences upon which to build a model for the concept of "normal." Sometimes they decide that normal is what their parents *don't* do, but that still leaves them with little understanding of what "normal" is.

14. They have difficulty completing projects.

Children of addicted parents do not receive consistent rewards for completing tasks. That leaves them feeling discouraged by life or about life.

Ollina was very happy. Today she had gotten her first paycheck for her first real job. It was only picking up papers at the hamburger joint, but it was a job. Now she would be able to buy that pretty sweater. She was so tired of hand-me-downs. Her own new sweater! She couldn't remember the last new thing she had had to wear. She tore open the envelope with trembling fingers; inside was a green check for $36.52. Wow, she could even buy the matching mittens. When she got home she could hardly wait to show it to her mother.

Mom said, "Here, Ollina, I'll take it to the bank and cash it for you."

Suddenly Ollina was afraid. She knew that Mom would buy pot with it, just as she did with the child-support money. She said, "No, Mom, I'll cash it."

Her mother grabbed the check and put it in her pocket, saying, "You've got to go to school tomorrow. When you get home, I'll have your money."

Ollina doubted that very much, but she could not bring herself to say anything but, "OK, Mom."

The next day every class seemed two hours long. When school was finally out Ollina ran home, but before she got to the door she knew it was too late. Uncle Bill's car was in the driveway, and she could hear the guitar playing and her mother laughing. Ollina knew she was stoned.

She slowly opened the door. Through the haze, she could see Uncle Bill and Mom sitting on the couch, passing a joint back and forth. All her mother said was, "So what are you looking at? Get your clothes changed. You've got a job, you know."

That evening Ollina quit her job.

Children of drug-abusing parents are usually very discouraged people. They have not had a chance to learn that hard work and diligence are rewarded.

15. They lie when it would be just as easy to tell the truth.

Holly's mother was high again. Holly could tell that she was in a good mood. Mom said, "Honey, I think I'm going to get a good job for a change. I'll make lots of money, and we'll have the biggest Christmas ever!"

"I know," Holly said, "and you can get me that big doll with the blue eyes. You're the best mom a kid could ever have."

Holly knew that her mother never kept the promises she made when she was high. Still, it was fun to pretend. It was the only chance she got to have fun with her. When Mom was coming down off speed, she was depressed, hateful, and abusive, sometimes violently so. But this part was fun.

Christmas came and went and there was no doll with blue eyes or any other presents. Back in school, Pam said, "Hey, Holly, what did you get for Christmas? I got a new sweater, Guess jeans, and a new doll."

Holly said, "I got a life-size doll with blue eyes and some new black Keds."

"Wear your Keds tomorrow, and I'll wear my Guess jeans."

Holly shook her head. "I gave my Keds to my cousin because she didn't get anything for Christmas."

"Wow, that was quite a sacrifice for you to make."

"Not really. Her dad's out of work, and I did get my doll."

"I'll come over after school and we can play dolls."

"No, you can't come over," Holly said quickly, "my mom's sick."

"Why don't you bring your doll and come over to my house?"

"I'll have to stay home and take care of Mom."

Kids with addicted parents find that lying is less painful than telling the truth. It eventually becomes a habit. So they lie even when telling the truth would be easier.

16. They have trouble having fun.

Jennifer and Jessie were playing cards. Jennifer laid down a Jack and Jessie laid down a Queen. Jessie said, "I win!"

"No, you don't," Jennifer insisted. "All face cards are worth ten points."

Jessie screamed, "Not in War. Mom, Jennifer's cheating again!"

Their mother had just dozed off when she heard that. Now she was angry when she came into the den. "What's wrong with you girls? You know I hate fighting. I'll teach you to fight!" and she slapped both of them and grabbed the cards, ripping them in half one at a time.

A week later Jennifer and Jessie were attending her funeral. Her suicide note said, "I never was any good as a mother. You will probably hate me for doing this. I never knew how to do anything right. Some people should just quit trying."

After the funeral Aunt Gladys said, "You will have to help your dad, now that your mom is gone." That surprised them because they had been doing Mom's job for years. So what else was new?

Kids with addicted parents are often overly mature. As if they missed adolescence, they seem to go from five to thirty-five years of age.

17. They take themselves too seriously.

After their mother's funeral, Jennifer and Jessie realized that their father was severely depressed. He stayed that way for the next eight months. That was when the girls went to his room and gave him a good talking-to. Jennifer said, "Dad, this is crazy. You've got a job, a house, a car, and us. It's time you went out and met a lady. That's what we want you to do."

Jessie said, "We've arranged to have Aunt Gladys stay with us so you can have some time out on your own."

The next week Jennifer tried out for the lead in the school play. She clearly had the best singing voice and she was cute, but the director said, "She's just too serious. This is a light, romantic comedy. She comes across like something from a Shakespearean tragedy."

Jennifer told him that he would regret his decision when she was a Hollywood movie star.

Jessie refused to go out for basketball that year, claiming that she had "more important responsibilities."

18. They have trouble establishing and maintaining intimate relationships.

Parents who use drugs repress almost all of their feelings except anger, and they insist that family members do likewise.

They repress feelings because they feel so bad about themselves. If they got in touch with any of their feelings, they would get in touch with all of them—and they couldn't handle that.

The result is that kids with drug-abusing parents end up expressing only thoughts and repressing feelings. That makes it very hard to establish intimate relationships. On those rare occasions when they do form a relationship with a minor level of intimacy, they distance themselves whenever the other person wants to talk about feelings. That almost always results in the end of the relationship.

Emil, almost twenty and a sophomore in college, was very depressed. He had begun to see signs, which he certainly recognized by now, that his girlfriend Patti was beginning to want out of the relationship. They had been dating for over a year, and lately he had begun to think that Patti was the girl he wanted to marry. But now Patti, like every other girl he had seriously dated, was beginning to be "busy" a lot of times when he called, seemed to go with girlfriends a lot of places that she used to go with him— oh, yes, he knew the signs well enough by now.

He could never have understood things from Patti's point of view. She liked him, too, liked him a lot. But whenever she wanted to talk about her feelings for him, and find out his feelings for her, suddenly it was as if he were in the next county. He more or less ignored what she was trying to communicate.

Since he could never discuss the subject of feelings, Patti could only conclude that Emil had no special feelings for her, despite the fact that he said he loved her. She would rather look for a guy who could express what he felt, who wouldn't just leave her dangling on their feelings for each other.

19. They overreact to changes over which they have no control.

Children who grow up with addicted parents try to control as much of their environment as possible. When a change takes place that they cannot control, they experience it as extremely stressful and usually overreact to it.

Paul was nine years old, from a family that was really messed up. When they were totally without money, Paul could usually manage to shoplift something that could be sold or pawned. He managed, somehow, to keep things under control.

One day he came home from school to find his mother

and little brothers sitting on the sidewalk with their belongings. The building had been condemned, his mother told him.

Paul started screaming, crying, and using dirty words. Things were out of control and he couldn't handle it.

But a shelter for homeless families took them in. The woman there was very kind and understanding. Everything seemed better.

A few days later Paul came home from school to discover that his family had been moved to other rooms. The woman in charge tried to explain that they needed to paint the first rooms the family had lived in. But Paul didn't listen; he was crying, screaming, and swearing.

20. They believe they are different from other people.

Although that is true is some respects, these children believe they are different in more ways than they really are. The primary reason is that they feel different.

Sherri was seventeen when her boyfriend told her that he felt "too tied down" and wanted to date other girls. Sherri had sort of expected it. Her father was always saying things like that to her mom. Sherri remembered the terrible fight her parents had had when she was only seven. She had waked up one night to hear her father shouting and her mother begging and crying, "Please don't leave! What about the children?"

"The hell with you and the hell with the kids. I'm going to move in with Jackie!" her father yelled.

So what else was new?

Her father had left several times, but he had always come back—at least until that last time.

Sherri was just like her mother. No boy would ever stay with her. But she wouldn't beg like her mother—no way was she ever going to do that.

"So to hell with you!" she shouted at her boyfriend, and suddenly realized how much like her father she sounded.

Children of addicted parents know only two roles in life —victim and victimizer. Both are painful. They are strangers to the healthy place between the two extremes that is called assertive, responsible behavior. To live and function in such a place, a teenager needs to feel a good deal of self-worth. These kids feel worthless and believe that they are no good.

21. They are extremely loyal, even when it is un-deserved.

These children have spent most, if not all, of their lives in families where loyalty is demanded but almost never deserved. As they mature, this accustomed way of living is transferred to other relationships.

Donna's mother was always on speed, either way up or way down. She was never emotionally available to Donna and her younger sister. Several times the social worker came to talk to Donna about her mother's drug use, but Donna always staunchly defended her, denying that anything was wrong.

Donna's English teacher was also her basketball coach. He often told off-color jokes in class and frequently swore during practice. And sometimes he seemed to be a little too free with his hands, once even fondling Donna's breasts.

The one thing Mr. Johnson did was to treat Donna "nicely"; that is, he talked kindly to her and didn't hit her. The principal called Donna to the office once to ask about the coach and whether he had done anything that seemed wrong to her.

"Oh, no!" Donna shook her head. "He's a great guy, the most wonderful coach in the world."

22. They are impulsive and don't consider the consequences of their decisions or alternative actions they could have taken.

Gina's mother gave her twenty dollars to buy groceries on the way home from school. During lunch break she and her best friend, Donita, went to the school bookstore.

"Look, Gina, the new school sweatshirts are out," Donita said excitedly.

"They're beautiful, and only eight dollars," Gina said enthusiastically. She decided to buy one; after all, Mom did owe her ten dollars in allowance money.

Donita said, "My dad will buy me one, but they'll all be gone by the time he gets back from his business trip. Will you lend me the money, Gina?"

"Sure," Gina said, digging in her purse.

At home that night Gina told her mother that she had had no other choice. Donita wanted a sweatshirt, and they would all have been gone. Gina never considered that her mother might not have another twenty dollars. She never thought about putting the sweatshirts on layaway. She acted on impulse.

That happens because people in addicted families learn to live for the moment, to get what pleasure they can right now, before things change and the opportunity is gone forever.

23. They have difficulty identifying and expressing their feelings.

It is not okay to have feelings in alcoholic families. To be more precise, only the alcoholic parent can have feelings, and the only one he or she usually expresses is anger. To express feelings could risk opening the door to the tremendous, gut-wrenching pain in which they all live. So the whole family repress their feelings. Eventually they don't even know what they do feel.

Mark wanted to try out for the basketball team, but he knew that Dad wanted him to work at the gas station after school, so he didn't show up. When the coach asked where he had been, he said, "Doing something useful."

The coach said, "But you told me you really wanted to try to make the team this year."

Mark shrugged and said, "I just changed my mind."

Two years later Mark's dog was run over right in front of him and his girlfriend Stephanie. Stephanie was terribly upset and crying, but Mark just took his dog's body to the backyard and buried it. Even so, he seemed depressed the next day. Stephanie asked what he was feeling. He replied, "I'm not really sure."

"Maybe you're upset about Spot."

Mark looked surprised. "I don't think so."

24. They believe they have no choice about the way they live their lives.

Kids in these families have been disappointed and discouraged all their lives. They think that they just don't matter.

James got a new bicycle for Christmas. It was the best bicycle he had ever seen—simply beautiful. He couldn't believe it.

Mom had actually kept her promise. She had made a bargain with him: She would put $50 down on the bike if he would earn the other $22.50. He had mowed lawns, picked up cans, baby-sat, and washed Mrs. Green's windows.

Now he had the bicycle, and it was even the color he wanted. He loved that bike. It was perfect. He rode it every single day for three weeks. Then one morning the bike was gone.

He looked everywhere, even reported it to the police, but it was hopeless. It was gone. Mom just said, "Maybe it will turn up," and she objected that he had called the cops. James hoped against hope that he would find it—at least, he hoped that until he overheard his mother telling his aunt, "The check bounced. I feel terrible, but I had to take it back."

James went to his room and cried and cried. "It's just like Dad's drinking," he thought. "I didn't have any control over that, either. I could never get him to stop. I wonder where he is now?"

"Hoping is for fools. Thinking things will ever get better is for idiots," James thought, as he drifted off to sleep.

25. They are rigid and controlling.

Young people who have addicted parents hate the fact that they can never count on their parents. They desperately want to be able to count on things being the same day in and day out.

When Jerry answered the knock on the door, he was surprised to see two policemen standing on the porch.

"Can I help you?" he asked, nervously.

One of them said, "Does May Johnson live here?"

"Yes, she's my mother."

"Is your father home?"

"I haven't seen my dad in years. Look, what's wrong?"

"Well, your mother has been in an accident and she's

been badly hurt, very badly. She's at Metropolitan Hospital."

The policemen called social services and placed Jerry and his sister in foster care. By the time his mother was well enough to come home, their apartment had been rented to another family. Jerry and his sister were never able to find out what had happened to their clothes, toys, and the only picture they had of their dad.

Jerry will always demand that people in his life behave pretty much the way *he* wants them to—for example, always be on time. He will do everything he can to be certain of it, including getting very angry when anyone else is late. He will even demand that other people keep the schedule he sets out for them. Some of his friends won't accept his need to be in control. He will reject those who won't go along.

26. They experience a pervasive sense of guilt.

These kids believe that their parents drink or use drugs partly because they are such bad kids. That is especially true of kids who have two addicted parents. Psychologically, it works like this: "I can't blame Mom because I love her, I can't blame Dad because I love him, so it must be all my fault."

Claire hated to hear her parents fight, hated the names they called each other, the things they said to each other. But they were at it again. When would it stop? Ever?

Finally she couldn't take it any more. "Please!" she begged, "can't you please stop? I'll do anything you want. I'll clean the house, I'll cook, I'll wash the dishes, I'll even wash the van. Just please stop!"

"Oh, shut up!" her father bellowed. "You're just like

your mother! You're a good-for-nothing tramp! Who'd want to eat anything you cooked?"

These young people will carry the scars of growing up in addicted homes for the rest of their lives. It will affect their lives, their marriages, their children. The pain and unhappiness will go on years beyond the time they leave their home and parents—unless they get treatment. To find out how to do that, read Chapter 13.

CHAPTER ◇ 11

Blowing the Whistle

Growing up in an addicted family is an endless
nightmare—no one needs to tell you that. But
there is a point at which it descends from
nightmare into hell itself, and that is when the addiction
fuels physical or sexual abuse. It changes legally here, too.
The law may tsk-tsk over children being raised by
alcoholics or dope users, but abuse crosses the line into the
patently and unacceptably illegal.

Children of such abuse are afraid to say anything for a
number of reasons. The simplest is knowing that when Dad
is bailed out of jail they'll get more of the same. The most
complex is that they do still love their parents.

Family loyalty—and remember they can be extremely
loyal—comes into play, too. And not always loyalty to the
abusing parent, either.

Jennifer had been molested by her father for over a year
before she finally broke down and told a teacher about it. "I
can't turn him in," she wailed tearfully. "He'd go to jail and
then what would happen to us? We barely get by as it is,
and Mom's so helpless I don't think she's capable of going
to the store for a loaf of bread by herself. You've got to
promise me you won't tell anyone!"

Unfortunately, Jennifer was right. Families certainly can and do wind up on welfare, homeless, when Dad goes to jail for such crimes.

The abuser often uses that fear to control his victim, to keep him or her from reporting the abuse. "If you tell, think what will happen. They'll separate all you kids, farm you out to foster homes; you'll never see each other again. Your mom will wind up on the streets. We'll lose the house."

Unfortunately, that scenario can be true. Social services people and the law itself have been known to be both heartless and brainless in the handling of such families, seeming to care more about guarding themselves against possible criticism than doing what is best for the emotional welfare of the children involved.

So this story doesn't—for now anyway—have a happy ending. That is simply one of the things that must be faced.

But you *must* tell someone for your own sake as well as the sake of brothers and sisters. The victims of such abuse have gone on to become prostitutes, murderers—and abusers themselves. *No one* walks away from such a situation without terrible emotional scars. And the sooner you walk away, the better.

But how can you do it with the least risk of everyone's life being torn apart? Sometimes you can't, but sometimes you can do something to make things better.

Recommending that you talk to your minister may be good advice, or it may not. Some ministers have training in dealing with emotional problems, and some don't. Some, in fact, might come totally unglued at hearing that your father is a sexual abuser. It probably boils down to using your own best judgment.

Some churches or denominations have facilities to help families—shelters, financial aid, etc. If a church agency is taking care of your family, it is possible that the law will not step in and make you wards of the court headed for foster homes.

The reason children are taken away from home in situations like this is that the police assume—usually correctly—that Mom had to know about it and made no effort to stop it. If Mom genuinely didn't know about it, there is a chance you could stay together.

Getting another relative to take over the family care is a possibility—an aunt, perhaps, or grandparents. Sometimes even an older brother or sister is considered mature enough to be a guardian, although that may be iffy. After all, they grew up with the same parents and might have been abused themselves.

If you have a relative or friend that you trust, talk to him or her before you talk to the law. Having someone go with you to the police station to assure that the family is being cared for may prevent anyone from stepping in too hastily to hustle everyone into some kind of "protective" situation.

All this certainly is not meant to make the legal process and the police sound like the enemy—someone to be feared. In this case the enemy is at home, not here. But everyone has heard horror stories, a lot of them are true, and the resulting fear keeps a lot of kids from telling what is happening to them.

That is something that social services people should understand: Bad as things are at home, they are at least a *known* factor. What will happen after the kid blows the whistle is not. The devil that you don't know is always more scary than the devil that you *do* know.

But blowing the whistle is necessary; it is the only way

you can protect yourself and your siblings and get your lives started in the right direction.

Sometimes blowing the whistle is not for your own sake, but for someone else's. Sexual abuse probably didn't begin with you, and it almost certainly will not end with you. The abuser will simply go on finding other victims, and often, especially when fueled by alcohol or drugs, he becomes more and more violent.

Case Study: Greta suffered sexual abuse from her step-father from age eleven until the day when, at fifteen, she decked him with a roundhouse punch and screamed, "If you ever touch me—or Michelle or Willa either—I'll kill you, so help me!"

After that she watched Ernie like a hawk and hovered over her little sisters. Even so, one day she caught him coming out of Michelle's room "with this funny look on his face. I said if I saw him near her one more time I was telling the cops."

In the library a few days later, working on a school assignment, Greta found a book on sexual molesters. She checked it out and read it and found that a lot of men are situational or opportunistic sexual abusers. If a victim is handy, they will abuse that victim, but they are unlikely to go hunting victims.

But for many men, especially if they drink heavily or use drugs, this becomes an accelerating pattern.

It usually begins with window peeping, sometimes before they are even in their teens. Next is molesting of friends and siblings, usually just touching and fondling at first. That becomes rape, with increasing force and violence; then it becomes murder, then serial murder like those committed by Ted Bundy.

"It scared me out of my wits," Greta recalls. "I had heard Ernie talk about peeping in windows when he was a kid; he thought it was funny. And I knew how much he drank. I always suspected that he used drugs, but I was never sure. That book really upset me, because I didn't know what to do—go to the police, tell Mom, or what. I didn't think Mom would believe me, but maybe if Michelle told her, too . . ."

Before Greta could make up her mind, one of Michelle's playmates was raped and murdered two streets over. When Greta heard about it she ran into the bathroom and threw up her breakfast.

"It was the most awful feeling in the world. I thought, Ernie did it—and it was all my fault!"

She sleepwalked through the school day like a zombie, then forced herself—"shaking so I could hardly stand up" —to go to the police station that night. There she learned that the murderer had been caught and had confessed—it wasn't Ernie! "But it could have been. It could have been Michelle or Willa he murdered, and I knew it! I *had* to go on and tell them."

It was pretty bad for Greta when she told. Her mother didn't believe her and slapped her right in front of the cops. But Willa backed up what she said, told her mom and the policewoman that Ernie came into her room at night . . .

Today Ernie is serving a long prison term and Greta, her mother, and both sisters are seeing a therapist. About blowing the whistle, Greta says, "I just wish I had done it sooner. Years before, in fact."

Now she can sleep, and she doesn't have to fear the sound of the bedroom door opening in the middle of the night. Neither does anyone else.

CHAPTER 12

The Recovery Process

R ecovery is a very complicated matter. On the most basic level, it involves reversing the psychological defenses employed to shield the addict against the emotional pain of his addiction. Those defenses are projection, blaming, displacement, rigidity, denial, minimization, repression of feelings, expression of anger, and blackouts with confabulation, the defenses described in Chapter 5, The Addicted Personality.

In a very real sense, recovery is a journey, or a series of journeys, from those defensive ways of dealing with the world to a healthier way of being.

The Journey from Projection to Experiencing

The defense of projection is used to overcome the necessity of facing the emotional pain of addiction. In recovery, the addict quits projecting and actually begins to experience emotional pain the way a normal person would experience it.

Case Study: Brooke's father was an alcoholic. He had been through treatment and had been attending Alcoholics

Anonymous for three years. He was also an only child whose mother had died several years earlier. His father was quite old and becoming more and more senile daily.

One Saturday morning Brooke and her father were working outside, Dad mowing and Brooke edging the yard, when her mother came out and talked quietly to Dad. Brooke could see that Mom was upset, so she went to find out what was wrong.

Her mother was saying, "The police have your father. They found him wandering around, lost and disoriented, about a mile from his house. He couldn't tell them where he lived. We've got to do something to protect him from himself."

Brooke's father looked sad as he said, "I know. We have to put him in a nursing home. And I promised him I would never do that."

Brooke saw his hands tremble and knew that he was going to cry. "I hate so much to have to do that."

"I know, honey," Mom said, hugging her husband and beginning to cry, too. Brooke hugged them both, and they stood like that for a long time. Then they went to the police station together.

Sad as it was, the family in general and Brooke's dad in particular were acting in a *normal* way, responding to the situation normally, not as they would have if Dad had still been drinking.

The Journey from Rigidity to Growth

The defense of rigidity is used to deal with the inability of the addict to handle change. The addict's mind does not handle change well at all.

In recovery, the addict experiences change as a normal

part of life. It is no longer feared as threatening. It may even be sought after.

Case Study: Brittany's father was addicted to speed. He had been in recovery for six years. He attended Narcotics Anonymous three times a week, working hard on his recovery. Mom attended AlAnon, and Brittany went to regular meetings of Alateen.

Dad had been working for the Bentac Corporation for eight years and was senior account manager. He had lived in Fort Worth all his life.

One evening during dinner the phone rang. It was for Brittany's dad. "This is he," he said. "Yes, I've heard a lot of good things about your company . . . in Chicago . . . the vice presidency? . . . How much? . . . Are you *serious*? Yes, of course I'm interested . . . but give me some time . . . I need to think about this and talk to my family . . . I'll have an answer for you by Friday." He hung up the telephone, looking a little like a man who's been clipped by an iron pipe.

"That was Cletus Brown, president of Control Graphics in Chicago—I told you about meeting him last week. He has offered me the vice presidency of his company. It would be a $25,000 a year increase in salary. But it would mean moving to Chicago." He looked around the table at the astonished faces. "What do you think?"

"Oh, Tom," his wife said. "That would mean so many changes! At least, now I can talk about being afraid."

Brittany said, "I'd hate to leave all my friends and school and everything, but it might be fun living someplace else for a while, and I could always come back here to college. When you think of it, I've lived in this one house all my life."

"I'd like to give it a try," Tom said. "I might never get an opportunity like this again!"

Mom said, "I'll be supportive and go along. It just might be fun. It certainly will be different—and a change."

Her father laughed and said, "I can't believe I'm looking forward to this!"

Once, even with the salary increase, the job offer would have been a frightening threat.

The Journey from Denial to Honesty

Denial is a defense used to avoid knowing the extent of one's addiction. Denial also protects the addict from knowledge of the damage that is being done to self and others by the addiction.

Case Study: Amanda's mother is an alcoholic who joined Alcoholics Anonymous eighteen months ago. Since then life has become more and more normal—and happy—for all the family.

One morning Amanda opened the door to find her mother's friend, Mary, on the doorstep. Mary belonged to a social club that Amanda knew, from past experience, served booze by the gallon at their parties. Now Mary was asking Amanda's mom to help serve at a party coming up the next weekend.

Mom shook her head. "Look, Mary, I know those parties, and I know myself. I didn't even plan to go to the party."

"But Blanche, surely just once . . ."

"I know with that bunch it's hard to get a soft drink or something nonalcoholic, and I'm not going to take the risk just now. Later, when I feel on firmer ground, we'll see.

But I'm afraid I'd start thinking that 'Just one drink won't hurt.' So, no, count me out."

When Mary had left—in a huff—Amanda raced to hug her mother. "I'm so proud of you, Mom. I was really afraid for a minute there . . ."

"Honey, so was I. That's why I said no. I've learned to be honest about and *with* myself and what I can and can't do."

The Journey from Blaming to Responsibility

The defense of blaming enables the addict to point a finger at someone else, thereby escaping responsibility for an irrational and damaging addiction. What the addict does not realize is that the very hand that points a finger at someone else has three fingers pointed backward right at the addict.

The author once received a notice from a car manufacturer saying, "A defect has been discovered in your model of car. Continued driving could result in injury or even death." The author was struck by the way fault was placed on the driver of the automobile, not the manufacturer who was ultimately responsible for the defect.

That is what the defense of blaming does. When an addict gets into recovery, he quits blaming and accepts responsibility for his own behavior.

Case Study: Brice's father is a recovering alcoholic. Life for all the family has been better and easier in the two years since he got treatment and joined Alcoholics Anonymous.

The family owns two rental houses. Over his mom's protests, Brice's dad had rented one of them to a cousin, even though the cousin had recently declared bankruptcy and had a long history of not working—not because he couldn't find a job but because he didn't look for one.

Five months later the cousin was three months behind on his rent and had been fired from two different jobs for absenteeism. He had also knocked a hole in a wall and broken two windows.

"What are we going to do now?" Brice's mom demanded. "That jerk is costing *us* a lot of money."

"I'm not sure," Dad said. "I'll tell him to move. I do know I made the decision, and I'll have to deal with the problem. It is my responsibility."

Brice remembers how at one time the responsibility for *any* problem in the family was enough to send his father into a binge.

The Journey from Displacement to Assertiveness

When an addict uses displacement as a psychological defense, he does so because he feels that he cannot confront the person with whom he is actually angry. That is because most addicts grew up with parents who were also addicts. In this sense they are very much like abused children who know only two roles: victim and victimizer.

They have experienced both of those roles. What they haven't experienced is that place in between, the healthy place called assertiveness. Assertiveness is not hostility. It is stating straightforwardly what one needs, wants, believes, and feels.

Case Study: Niki's mother went into treatment for alcoholism six months ago, and for Niki it has been like having a new person around the house. The most notable difference is that Niki is no longer the target of her mother's rages when things don't go well at work.

Mom works for a man who has a strong streak of sadistic bully in him. Nothing that goes wrong in the office is ever his fault. He takes out his temper on Niki's mom, who then used to spend the evening yelling at Niki, her father, and her big brother.

After treatment, the first time her boss threw a tantrum Niki's mom said, "Mr. Schneider, if you don't want mistakes in your letters, don't dictate them while you are trying to eat a doughnut. And don't yell at me again. You can treat me like an adult who is good at my job, or you can get another secretary."

The boss was so astonished that he spilled coffee down the front of his shirt, Mom was happy to note.

The next time he yelled at her Niki's mother went to *his* boss, explained the situation, and said, "I like working for this company, and I want very much to stay. But if you can't find me another opening, I'm leaving. I refuse to be that man's emotional lightning rod any longer." The boss's boss moved her to another department.

Mom also apologized to Niki and the rest of the family. "I was doing the same thing to you that Schneider was doing to me—I just didn't realize it." Niki loved hearing the story. To her, Mom seemed like a heroine.

The Journey from Expression of Anger to Leveling

Addicts most often employ the psychological defense of expression of anger in order not to deal with the pain of a life that is out of control.

The persons closest to an addict are the very ones most often victimized by the addict's anger. Such a small thing as a daughter's saying, "Do you want to see my class picture?" can trigger an explosion: "Do you think that's all I've got to do with my time? You sit around all day in school flirting with boys while I work my behind off to support you and that lazy good-for-nothing mother of yours. You're no good, just like her! Why don't you do something useful for a change, like cook dinner or do the laundry?"

Of course, *not* showing Dad the school picture could just as easily have drawn, "Didn't bother to show me your school picture, huh? What's the matter, I'm not important enough? Is that it? You'll show other people, but don't bother with the person who works his butt off so you can pay for things like that . . ." The child of an addict can't win, no matter what he or she may do.

What the addict is feeling is stress. If he were to level with his daughter, or the world in general, there would be a real chance of getting the help he needs.

Case Study: Celeste's father was a heroin addict. He had had only two months of being straight, but he was really working the Narcotics Anonymous program. His sponsor had reommended that he attend ninety meetings in ninety days. He was also working as much overtime as possible to pay his hospital bill for treatment. He had almost no time to himself. In the past any request for time would have triggered an irrational outburst of anger.

Celeste wanted to ask him to come to the Homecoming football game. She was also very much afraid to ask. Still, he was behaving so differently since treatment that she decided to take the risk. "Dad, would you come to the game this Saturday? It's Homecoming, and I am first runner-up to the homecoming queen."

"I know, and I'm very proud of you," Dad said. "I'd like very much to go, but I just can't. The only meeting I can attend is during the game. I'm too new at being off that garbage to risk falling back now. I'll miss being there, and I'll be thinking about you."

Celeste did miss her dad at the game, but somehow she

felt right about his not being there. He had leveled with her, and he was working hard to stay straight.

The Journey from Minimization to Acceptance

The defense of minimization is usually employed by the addict in an effort to avoid painful realization of life. In recovery, the addict begins to accept himself as a human being who sometimes makes mistakes. Mistakes are accepted as part of life. Making mistakes doesn't mean he is bad, only human. Acceptance means that he is less judgmental of others.

Case Study: Teresa's mom had been addicted to a variety of drugs. She had gone through treatment and aftercare and was currently active in Narcotics Anonymous. A single parent, she has been straight for almost two years.

On vacation Teresa and her mom went to the mountains about five hundred miles from home. Teresa was in charge of reading the map, and her mother drove.

Everything seemed to go wrong. The road got worse and worse, narrow and full of holes. Then it just ended, running out in a patch of pine trees in sandy-looking ground.

Teresa's mom said, "Do you have any idea where we are?"

"Well—I'd say lost. I'm sorry, Mom. I *thought* I knew where we were."

"Well, we'll just have to go back to someplace we recognize and try again." But as Mom tried to turn the car the rear wheels slipped off into the deep sand and got stuck.

After a few minutes of trying to get the car out and realizing they couldn't, Mom said, "I guess we'll just have to walk out and get help."

Teresa began to cry. "Oh, Mom, I'm so sorry. It's all my fault." Once Mom would have agreed with that, and probably at the top of her lungs. Now she laughed and tousled Teresa's hair. "Don't be silly, honey. You got us lost, and I got us stuck. I'll rest a lot easier when we reach civilization and get someone to pull us out of this mess, but the walking out will be an adventure. After all, what's a camping trip for but adventure?"

The Journey from Confabulation to Admission

Confabulation is the defense employed to deal with the fear of insanity caused by blackouts from excessive drug or alcohol use.

Episodes of amnesia are extremely frightening. Most addicts fear that they are losing their mind. Everyone knows exactly where the addict was and what he or she did and said—except the addict. It is especially scary when the addict was sober.

Addicts react to that fear by "filling in the blanks" or inventing a story of where they were, what they did, and what they said. That is confabulation.

In recovery, the addict admits that he or she has no memory of things that occurred during the blackouts. The good news is that in recovery blackouts happen less and less frequently until for most addicts they subside altogether.

Case Study: Rose's dad was addicted to cocaine, marijuana, and alcohol. He had been through treatment twice. This time it seemed to be working. He had been sober and straight and attending Narcotics Anonymous for three months. He still experienced blackouts, but they were further apart and shorter than in the beginning.

One morning he told Rose not to take the bus after school because he would pick her up and take her to visit her grandmother that evening. When school let out, Rose waited for her father—who did not show up. After half an hour she went to the principal's office and called him. "Why didn't you come and get me?" she asked.

He sounded blank on the other end of the line. "Why didn't you take the bus?"

"You told me that you were going to pick me up and we were going to Grandmother's."

"I said that? Oh—baby, I'm so sorry! I guess I've had another blackout. I'll come and get you right away. I wonder if I told your grandmother, or *what* I told her. I'll call her as soon as I pick you up."

The Journey from Repression of Feelings to Intimacy

Addicts repress all feelings except anger because getting in touch even with positive feelings also gets them in touch with the pain of addiction. In recovery, they learn once again to express the full range of emotions. That leads to the development of intimate relationships.

Case Study: Martin's mother was addicted to Zanex, a prescription drug. She had been in recovery for two and a half months.

She hadn't cried since she was a teenager. She wasn't even sure if she still could cry. In fact, she didn't feel much of anything—not sadness, not happiness, not even love. She wondered if she ever would feel anything again.

She had started using Valium when she was thirteen and

switched to Zanex when she was thirty. The years between seemed to her a sort of sleepwalk. She had gone through them like a robot, seeing everything but feeling nothing. As a result, there was an enormous emotional distance between herself and her husband and children.

Martin and his mother were washing his dad's car, as a surprise for him. Their dog Hershey (Martin had named him Hershey because he was always giving kisses) was playing in the water and around their feet. When they started to dry the car, Hershey grabbed the towel and ran toward the street, with Martin in hot pursuit.

But Hershey ran right into the path of a car coming around the corner and was hit. Martin and his mother both screamed and ran to scoop him up. "Please, take us to the veterinarian's office!" Mom asked the driver of the car, which had stopped.

"Of course. Get in."

In the car Martin's mom was astonished to realize that she was holding Hershey and petting him—and crying.

It seemed like an eternity while they waited at the vet's office. Then the doctor came out with a big grin on her face. "He's going to be stiff and sore for a while, but no major damage was done. He'll be just fine."

They all hugged each other and laughed and cried— Martin, his mom, the vet, and the stranger who had been driving the car.

Only later did Martin's mother realize how odd it was that she had had to learn, all over again, to feel the emotions felt by the stranger—who had never seen any of them *or* Hershey before.

When they got home they laughed when they saw that Martin's dad had awakened from his Saturday afternoon nap and was standing in the driveway staring at his water-spotted car and the water running down the street because no one had thought to shut it off.

Martin's mother hugged him and said, "I know this may sound silly, but I've never felt more in love with you than I do at this minute."

At first Dad looked confused; then he smiled and hugged her back and said, "I've waited a long time to hear you say that. You don't know how good it sounds."

His parents went into the house, and Martin began to rewash the car—dancing and singing as he worked.

CHAPTER 13

Getting Help

T he best way to begin the process of getting help for an addicted parent is to call a chemical dependency treatment center or a certified drug and alcohol counselor.

Tell him or her that you have a parent who is addicted. The counselor will probably ask some questions, mainly why you think your parent is an addict. Once he or she is satisfied that you are right, an appointment will probably be made for you to come in to talk with the counselor.

It is possible that he or she will try to arrange an intervention.

The Intervention

Intervention is a technique designed to break through the addict's denial and to get him or her to accept the help that is so desperately needed.

It takes a lot of coordination and effort to arrange an effective intervention. First you need to tell the counselor the names and telephone numbers of other people who are interested in getting your addicted parent to quit, whether your parent works, and where. That will probably end the first interview.

During the next week, the counselor will call all of the people on the list and ask them to come to the next appointment. He or she will probably also check to see what kind of drug and alcohol treatment policy your parent's employer has. Many employers give employees time off without penalty for addiction treatment. Often, the parent's boss wants to be part of the intervention.

If the employer has no such policy, the counselor asks questions such as, "If you had an employee who was alcoholic or addicted, how would you deal with it?" to discover whether or not the employer will be helpful.

If it develops that the employer in fact will be helpful and genuinely cares about your parent, the counselor may invite him to participate in the intervention.

Next the counselor trains those who are to take part in the intervention. It is important that the confrontation be loving, a genuine attempt to *help* because everyone concerned cares about the addicted one.

A hostile confrontation would only raise the addict's defenses, making drug or alcohol use worse and genuine help less likely.

On the day of the intervention, all of the participants gather together. This usually takes place at the therapist's office or at the addict's workplace or home. Almost certainly the addict is surprised and, at first, not at all pleased.

The counselor says something on the order of, "Bill, we are all here today because we care about what's happening to you. We would like you to sit down and listen. You can talk after we've each had a turn."

Each person then says something like, "I love you, but this is what I've noticed." He or she states the problem behaviors, each time blaming the drugs, not the addict. After everyone has spoken, the counselor says, "Now each of us will tell you what we think needs to happen for you, and what we need for ourselves if you don't take our advice."

Then each person says, "Bill, you need to get treatment. If you don't, I will _____" Since all have different needs, they fill in the blank differently. For instance, the addict's wife may say, "I will divorce you." The boss may say, "I will fire you." The sister may say, "I won't welcome you in my home anymore."

Usually, with his support system folding up under him, the addict accepts treatment. At that point, he or she is taken immediately to a chemical dependency treatment center.

The Chemical Dependency Treatment Center

Chemical dependency treatment centers are hospitals for addicts. They may be part of a larger hospital, or separate units.

Usually treatment takes about a month. It consists of lectures, therapy (group, individual, and family), forced assignments, and attendance at self-help groups (discussed later in this chapter).

An important part of the treatment program is family week, usually held during the third week. The entire family is asked to participate in treatment. Some studies show that success rates climb from 33 percent to 85 percent when the family participate. Some centers make family participation a requirement of treatment.

After family week the addict, his counselor, and other treatment staff arrive at a discharge plan. The plan may have many elements, including such things as a change of employment or living situation. It may include continued family therapy.

It will certainly include aftercare and attendance at self-help groups for the family.

Aftercare

Most treatment centers require attendance at aftercare for the addict and perhaps for the family. Aftercare, a therapy group run by a drug and alcohol counselor, usually meets once a week after work. Its purpose is to continue working through issues that were not completed during hospitalization and to help the addict and his or her family to adjust to new ways of being together.

Self-Help Groups

These groups are often called twelve-step groups because they employ twelve steps to help members deal with problems. These groups are:

Alcoholics Anonymous (AA) for alcoholics.
Narcotics Anonymous (NA) for drug addicts.
Cocaine Anonymous (CA) for cocaine addicts.
AlAnon for the addict's spouse.
Alateen for the addict's teenagers.
Alatot for the addict's children.
Adult Children of Alcoholics (ACA) for adult children of alcoholics.
Children of Alcoholics (CA) for children of addicts.

If you live in a community that does not have the group best suited for you (Cocaine Anonymous, for example, is difficult to find in rural areas), attend one of the others.

It is very important that the addict *and* his or her family regularly attend a self-help group.

White-Knuckle Sobriety

Sometimes an addict decides to quit using a mood-altering chemical on his or her own. The addict intends to do so by the strength of his own willpower and without getting treatment or working through the twelve steps to recovery.

That never works!

The first of the twelve steps is the addict's admission of powerlessness over the mood-altering substance or behavior. When an addict tries to achieve recovery by his own power, all he gets is sobriety—not recovery.

Called "dry drunk sobriety," it means that the addict has quit using but all of the addictive defenses are still in place. In other words, the addict still has an addicted personality even though he is not practicing the addiction.

At Alateen meetings you may hear a depressed kid say, "Well, Dad has quit drinking, but it sure hasn't changed the way he acts. He's still a monster around the house, yelling and screaming at all of us . . ." Almost certainly that is what is going on. Dad is hanging on so tight that his knuckles have turned white.

Most of these people eventually begin practicing their addiction again. Those who don't are usually miserable for the rest of their lives—and so are their families.

What If My Addicted Parent Won't Get Help?

If you have tried everything and your parent or parents refuse to get help, *get help for yourself.* Attend Children of Alcoholics or Alateen. You can work on your own recovery even if your parent won't work on his. It won't be easy. You may even be forbidden to go "because it will make someone think we have a problem in this family and we *don't*!" But it can be done.

Read the literature on children of alcoholics. There are many books on this topic that can be very helpful to you. You will learn that other kids growing up with an addicted parent feel and think an awful lot like you.

That in itself can be healing to you. One of the problems of trying to cope with an addicted parent is the emotional isolation, the feeling of being alone, the feeling that you are the only kid in the world who has ever had to deal with something like that.

Make an appointment with your school counselor to talk about your parents' addiction and how it is affecting you. More and more school counselors are aware of these issues and have been trained to help.

CHAPTER ◇ 14

Living with What
You Can't Change

S ometimes, no matter how hard you try to make a difference, one or both of your parents will continue to practice his or her addiction.

When that happens the question quickly becomes, "How can I live with this?" It is an extremely important question. The majority of addicts do continue to practice their addiction until it kills them. So learning to live with it may be your only alternative.

Learning to live with addicted parents may be the most difficult challenge any child or adolescent ever has to face. It is important for you to understand that your actions will have a tremendous impact upon your ability to survive the experience in the most positive way possible. Here are some do's and don'ts.

DO'S

1. *Find friends who are healthy.* One or two good friends can make a big difference in your being able to release some of the stress under which you live. You will be able to share feelings openly, and that is productive for your growth as a person.

Remember that in addicted families members usually repress emotions and feelings. It is extremely important for you to develop outlets to express your feelings freely.

Other characteristics of healthy friendships are tendencies toward honesty, loyalty, equality, consideration, and kindness.

2. *Start a journal or diary.* Developing the habit of writing regularly in a journal can be extremely helpful.

There are several methods of keeping a journal. One method is simply to note the important events of each day. Another method is to address each entry to a particular person—a friend, a relative, or the person who plays the greatest role in that entry. Recount the events of the day or incident, then be sure to express how you felt during those events.

3. *Visit your school counselor.* Most school counselors are professionals who are trained to help students deal with the difficulties of life in general and living with addicted parents in particular. They can help you get a new perspective on your problems.

Be willing to attend enough sessions so that you and the counselor can get to know each other. It can be frightening to think about baring your soul to someone you hardly know, but participating in counseling can be an extremely enriching experiencing.

4. *Attend Alateen.* Few experiences are more healing than particpating in Alateen meetings. There you will find other

teens just like you in addicted families. It is very healing to share your worst fear—believing yourself to be the only person in the whole world who has that fear—only to have two other teenagers say, "I've been afraid of the same thing."

Alateen is called a Twelve-Step Recovery Program because the focus is on helping people work through to a place of health. If you attend Alateen meetings regularly and sincerely work the program, your rewards will be great.

5. *Make a list of all your good points.* (If you need to, get a good friend to help you.) Most children growing up in addicted families have very low self-esteem. It is usually very hard for them to realize that they do have good points. Making a list of them can be very enlightening. Many teenagers find it much easier to make a list of their bad points. But in the author's experience teens growing up in addicted family systems have a tremendous number of strengths that other teens don't have. For example, they are usually able to cope with crisis, they are survivors, and they are very self-sufficient. Making a list of your good points will help you to maintain a healthy balance within yourself.

6. *Call a Certified Drug and Alcohol Counselor.* If you can find a Certified Drug and Alcohol Counselor who is willing to spend some time talking to you on the phone about your problems, you may be able to get answers to many of the things that mystify you about your family.

Most of these counselors have either lived with an addicted person or been addicted themselves. They know the problems from personal experience. Most of them will be glad to talk to you.

7. *Arrange for an intervention.* When you talk to the Certified Drug and Alcohol Counselor, ask about the

possibility of arranging an intervention for your addicted parent. First read Chapter 10 of this book and make a list of questions you would like the counselor to answer.

An intervention is designed to get your addicted parent into treatment as soon as possible. An intervention could work for your parent, and the counselor will probably be glad to help you with it. If not, he will refer you to someone who can. A successful intervention could dramatically improve your whole family system.

8. *Attend a summer camp.* It can be helpful to have a break from living with an addicted parent. If you are able to attend summer camp, it could provide much needed relief. Most summer camps have trained counselors on staff. Be sure to seek them out and talk to them about the problems in your family.

Although the cost of summer camp can be prohibitive, scholarships are often available. Ask the organization that is advertising the camp you wish to attend.

9. *Participate in church or synagogue.* Regular participation in religious organizations can be helpful. Most pastors, priests, and rabbis entered the clergy because they wanted to be helpful to others. They would welcome the opportunity to talk with you. In addition, most religious organizations have youth programs and youth leaders who take an interest in teenagers.

Perhaps most important, you will have an opportunity to develop a strong faith relationship with God. Many adolescents growing up in addicted family systems have felt abandoned by everyone but God. Developing this relationship can make a great difference in how you deal with stress.

10. *Find a hobby you enjoy.* Collecting stamps, coins, marbles, dolls, insects, baseball cards or whatever can help you focus your mind, energy, and emotions on something

outside of the family problems. Activities such as sewing, making home movies, taking pictures, operating a Citizens Band radio, star-gazing, or building model airplanes can be a great diversion. A bonus of pursuing a hobby can be finding new friends with similar interests.

11. *Participate in sports.* Such games as basketball, football, baseball, soccer, tennis, and volleyball can be a great way to get involved with people your age. Team sports help to develop discipline, cooperation, and identification with a team effort toward a common goal.

Nonteam sports such as bicycling, swimming, diving, hiking, jogging, and weight lifting can also take your mind off your problems and increase your physical well-being. Activities such as band, pep club, and chorus may also serve this purpose.

12. *Join a youth organization.* The numerous youth organizations include Scouts, Campfire, Big Brothers, Big Sisters, 4-H, FFA, and church youth groups.

The benefits of participating in a youth organization include focusing your energy outside the home, gaining a commitment and sense of belonging to something outside of yourself, and helping you to maintain objectivity about your life.

13. *Visit with relatives.* One of the aspects of our society before the Industrial Revolution was that most of the members of the extended family (aunts, uncles, cousins, and grandparents) lived close to each other. That made visiting easy. Teenagers were able to benefit from relationships with older cousins, aunts, uncles, and especially grandparents. One way for this to happen today is for teenagers to make extended visits to favorite relatives. It can also help in keeping a perspective on your problems at home.

DON'TS

1. *Don't make excuses for your addicted parents.* That only protects them from the consequences of their behavior. Every time you excuse a parent for being drunk by saying, "Oh, he's been under a lot of stress at work lately," you only provide another reason to get drunk the next time he is under stress. Every time you lie to a parent's employer by saying, "Dad's sick and can't come to work today," only insures that the employer will have a harder time confronting your father for being too drunk to work.

These actions are called enabling behaviors because they allow an addicted person to continue practicing his addiction. It is far better to stop all enabling behaviors, thereby allowing the addict to suffer the consequences of his behavior.

2. *Don't try to "fix" your parent.* Trying to fix an addicted parent doesn't work for many reasons. The first is because it isn't your job. It is a parent's job to fix himself.

The second reason is that it is based on faulty logic. It is not your fault that your parent is addicted. If you try to fix your parent you well may end up accepting major responsibility for his condition or actions. Remember, your parent is addicted becuase he has inherited a genetic tendency to addiction.

The third reason that you shouldn't try to fix your parent is that teenagers tend to become overly involved in their parents' lives, thus losing a large part of their own lives. Children need to be children, and teenagers need to be teenagers. You only experience this time of your life once!

3. *Don't attack or criticize an addicted parent.* Remember that addicts have a very rigid defense system. When criticized, they first respond by feeling guilty. Then almost immediately they become defensive and begin to

rationalize and justify their addictive behavior. Criticism merely deepens their defense mechanisms and eventually leads to a higher level of addiction.

It is best to talk to an addict about what *you* feel. Start by saying, "I feel sad, alone, left out, etc." In that way the addict may be able to hear what your pain is about and not take it personally.

4. *Don't blame the addicted parent.* Blame the mood-altering drug or behavior. The addicted parent did not choose to be addicted; he was predisposed to become addicted. Thus blaming the drug or the behavior gives the addict the possibility of looking at the drug or behavior as the culprit. When he is less filled with guilt, he may be able to be more objective. That could be the first step toward his seeking help for his addiction.

5. *Don't experiment with mood-altering drugs or behaviors.* Remember, if one of your parents has a genetic predisposition toward addiction, you probably have it too. Some teenagers are absolutely defenseless against addiction. An example is type "A" alcoholism, which is passed down from father to son. It is characterized by early, frequent, and excessive drinking episodes. These boys usually begin drinking between the ages of eleven and thirteen, in some cases even earlier. They become addicted almost immediately. They often have long police records characterized by violence when drinking. By the time they are fourteen or fifteen they have developed such a tolerance for alcohol that they "drink their friends under the table."

Type "B" alcoholism can be passed down from either mother or father to daughter or son. The type "B" alcoholic usually starts drinking later and takes longer to become addicted.

6. *Don't set up your own abuse.* Many addicts are

violent. Those who are not are often verbally abusive. If you know that a certain behavior will set your parent into a sequence of abuse, avoid that behavior.

If you take time to think, you may be able to forestall much of your own emotional, or physical pain. It may not be easy to identify which of your actions or words sets up the abuse. For instance, some addicts become abusive when a son or daughter seems to cower, whereas others react when a son or daughter stands up to them. Once you figure out what sets the abusive cycle in motion, you will have much more power to prevent it.

7. *Don't wallow in self-pity.* Although you may have plenty of reason to feel sorry for yourself, it seldom accomplishes anything more than further lowering your self-image. It is better to focus on positive possibilities. Giving energy to the negative forces in your life gives them power. If you focus on the positive things in your life, you give them power. Like energy attracts like energy. Concentrate on the positive side of life. Don't fuel the negative aspects any more than necessary.

Just as there are do's and don'ts in dealing with the addiction of your parents, there are also things you need to do to avoid your own addiction and, eventually, the addiction of your children.

By now it should be clear to the reader that addiction is inherited, not developed. It is also clear that children of addicts have a host of emotional difficulties developed by growing up with an addicted parent. These emotional problems are passed on from generation to generation.

Given these facts, the thoughtful reader may be wondering about several issues: How can I avoid being addicted? Can I drink socially? Will I marry an addict? Will my children be doomed to repeat my parents' addiction problems? What about their children? Are any of us truly safe?

Will I Become Addicted?

If one of your parents is an addict, you have a 50 percent chance of becoming an addict. If both of your parents are addicts your odds could be as high as 75 percent. If your father was addicted at a very young age, was violent when drinking, and you are a male, your odds are as high as 90 percent. In fact, some people are absolutely defenseless against addiction from the moment they first use a mood-altering chemical. For many of you, your only defense against addiction is never to use or drink.

That makes it very important to discover whether anybody in your family either now or in the past is or was addicted. Since you are reading a book about drug-addicted parents, the answer may be obvious. But even if you are reading merely for information, you could end up addicted if a grandparent or great grandparent was addicted.

It operates like heredity in breeding animals. If a white dog and a black dog are mated, the outcome is usually one white puppy, one black puppy, and two black-and-white puppies. If the black puppy grows up and mates with a black dog, they may have three black puppies and one black-and-white puppy. If we compare the white puppy to a person in a human family, that white or alcoholic trait could show up generations later. Therefore, if you have had an addict in the family you should never drink or use a mood-altering chemical.

Even if you never use a mood-altering chemical, there is still a good possibility that you will pass on the genetic potential toward addiction to your children, and they will pass it on to theirs. You should help make sobriety a way of life in your family.

When you have children, you should start to educate them very early. It is known that 33 percent of all fourth-graders feel under pressure to use a mood-altering chemical, and 50 percent of all sixth-graders feel so pressured. So develop a drug-free life-style that involves healthy ways of feeling good about yourself.

This is crucial for you and all of your potential offspring, now and forever. You should practice total abstinence from mood-altering drugs.

Bibliography

Ackerman, Robert J. *Growing in the Shadow*. Pompano Beach, FL: Health Communications, 1986.

Annomimos. *The Twelve Steps*. San Diego: Recovery Publications, 1987.

Black, Claudia. *It Will Never Happen to Me*. MAC, 1982.

Brooks, Cathlene. *The Secret Everyone Knows*. Operation Cork, CA, 1981.

Gravits, Herbert L., and Bowden, Julie D. *Guide to Recovery*. Holmes Beach, FL: Learning Publications, 1985.

Kathleen W. and Jewell E. *With Gentleness, Humor and Love*. Deerfield Beach, FL: Health Communications, 1989.

Larsen, Ernie. *Old Patterns, New Truths*. New York: Harper/Hazelden, 1988.

Leite, Evelyn, and Espeland, Pamela. *Different Like Me*. Minneapolis: Johnson Institute, 1987.

Porterfield, Marie Porter. *Coping with an Alcoholic Parent*. New York: Rosen Publishing Group, 1985.

Weyscheider, Sharon. *Another Chance: Hope and Help for the Alcoholic Family*. Palo Alto: Science and Behavior Books, 1983.

―――. *Learning to Love Yourself*. Deerfield Beach, FL: Health Communications, 1987.

―――. *The Miracle of Recovery*. Deerfield Beach, FL: Health Communications, 1989.

Woilitz, Janet G. *Adult Children of Alcoholics*. Hollywood, FL: Health Communications, 1983.

Index

A

abandonment, fear of, 65,
121–122
abstinence, 8, 12, 169
abuse
child, 20, 67
emotional, 114
physical, 45, 114, 119, 136
sexual, 10–11, 45, 114,
122–123, 136–139
verbal, 95, 100, 167
acceptance, need for, 113–114
addiction, 1–25
chances of, 168–169
course of, 47–49
teenage, 21–22
addictive process, 15, 18
aftercare, 149, 157
Adult Children of Alcoholics
(ACA), 157
AlAnon, 143, 157
Alateen, 61, 88–90, 143, 157,
158, 159, 161–162
Alatot, 157
alcohol, 4, 7, 12, 13, 16, 22,
30–31, 38, 47, 139, 151
alcoholic, 2–5, 7–8, 12, 17,
21–22, 51–52, 65–66, 67,
68, 71, 76, 84, 86, 88, 97,
100, 110, 115, 119,
141–142, 144

alcoholic personality syndrome,
22
Alcoholics Anonymous, 22, 61,
141–142, 144, 145, 157
alcoholism, types of, 166
amphetamines, 24, 26
anger, 10–11, 19, 22, 23, 41, 60,
100, 114, 127
expression of, 51, 55–56, 132,
141, 151
moving to leveling,
148–149
anxiety, 23, 33, 36, 37, 38, 39,
40, 48, 76–77, 83

B

Bad Blood, 84
barbiturates, 24, 38
beer, 2–3, 16–17, 24, 31, 52
behavioral stage, of addiction,
47, 48–49
behavior
coaddictive, 76
controlling, 17, 22, 63, 68–69,
82, 133
mood-altering, 3, 5, 17
binge addict, 8–9, 24, 55–56,
101
blackout, 31, 47, 51, 56–57,
141, 150–151
blaming, 51, 54–55, 115, 141

avoidance of, 166
moving to responsibility,
    145–146
blowing the whistle, 136–138
brain damage, 22, 28, 31, 32, 34,
    35, 36
breakdown, emotional, 34, 35

C
capsules, as drug vehicle, 27, 28,
    29, 30, 33
caretaking, 63, 69–70
central nervous system, 15, 27
chemical stage, of addiction,
    47–48
children
    affected by addiction, 10–12,
        22, 39, 43–45, 59–61, 67,
        107
    friends of, 84–90, 161
    help for, 11–12, 61
    parenting siblings, 109–111
Children of Alcoholics (CA),
    157, 158–159
chronic stage, of addiction, 47,
    49
clown, family, 91, 99
coaddiction, 23, 62–83, 91
cocaine, 5, 12–14, 24, 28–29,
    31, 39, 64, 78, 79, 87, 92,
    94, 107, 151
    pure, 15–16
Cocaine Anonymous (CA), 157
coma, 15, 30, 82
computer, family, 91, 96–97
confabulation, 51, 56–57, 141
    moving to admission,
        150–151
control, loss of, 6, 17, 24, 48, 60

convulsions, 28
counselor
    Certified Drug and Alcohol,
        46, 154, 162
    outpatient, 14
    school, 159, 161
crack, 5, 15, 28, 36, 39
crank, 39, 40
crime, 20, 80
crystal, 28, 36, 39, 41
cure, myth about, 12, 24
cycle
    addictive, 37–45
    coaddict, 75–76

D
daily addict, 8–9, 24
defense mechanisms, 51–61,
    166
    reversing, 141–153
delirium tremens (DT), 31
denial, 44, 51–52, 63, 67, 141,
    156
    moving to honesty, 144–145
dependence, 65–66, 121–122
depressants, 29–32, 36
depression, 10–11, 23, 28, 33,
    34, 36, 37, 39, 40, 41, 55,
    121, 126, 127–128, 132
diabetes, 4, 18, 103
diplomat, family, 91, 106–107
disease
    addiction as, 17–18, 46–50
    liver, 31, 36
    lung, 32
displacement, 51, 53–54, 141
    moving to assertiveness,
        146–147
distractor, family, 91, 95–96

divorce, 18, 20, 88, 95–96, 104, 110
doctor-shopping, 23–24
downer cycle, 38–39, 40–41
drug of choice, 17, 36
drugs
  cutting, 15
  death from, 6, 15, 28, 29, 30, 31, 33, 49
  distribution of, 15–16
  prescription, 13, 23–24, 152
  selling, 1
  switching, 13–14
drunk driving, 2, 8, 22, 105
dry drunk sobriety, 158

E
enabling, 81, 165
endorphin, 4
ethyl alcohol, 31
etiology, of addiction, 47
euphoria, 5, 28, 30, 34, 35
excitement, addiction to, 117–118

F
family
  affected by addiction, 9–10, 62–83, 85, 120–121
  conflict in, 100–101, 106, 107–108
Fatal Vision, 27
fear
  of abuse, 138
  of anger, 114–115
  of authority, 112–113
feelings
  denying, 119–120
  of difference, 129–130

expressing, 131–132
repression of, 22, 51, 55, 97, 127, 141, 161
  moving to intimacy, 151–152
flashback, 22, 34, 42–43
freebase, 28

G
genetic predisposition, 3–4, 15, 17, 24, 47, 166, 168
guilt, feelings of, 37, 38, 39, 40, 42, 60, 76–77, 78, 82, 114–115, 134, 166

H
hallucinations, 22, 28, 34, 35
hallucinogens, 32, 42–43
hashish, 33
heart attack, 15, 16
help
  availability of, 18
  seeking, 19, 22, 148, 154–159
hero, family, 91–92
heroin, 13–14, 98, 115, 148
homicide, 33, 50
honesty, 14, 161

I
ice, 28
impulsiveness, 131
inhalant, 22, 24, 35–36
injection, drug, 27, 28, 29, 30, 34
interpersonal boundaries, 63–63
intervention, 154–156, 162–163
irrevelant child, 91, 105–106
isolation, feeling of, 44, 84, 112–113, 159

J
jealousy, 48, 49, 77
journal, keeping, 161

L
Levine, Richard M., 84
lost child, 91, 97–98
love, 11
    confused with pity, 118–119
    family, 10–11
loyalty, 130–131, 136, 161
lying
    habitual, 124–125
    to self, 7
lysergic acid diethylamide
        (LSD), 2, 22, 34, 42

M
mainlining, 27, 115
marijuana, 1, 5, 13, 32–33, 54,
        57, 151
martyr, family, 91, 102
mascot, family, 91, 98
McGuinness, Joe, 27
memory loss, 17, 31, 32, 33
mescaline, 34–35
methadone, 30
minimization, 51, 53, 141
    moving to acceptance,
        149–150
mood swings, 34, 35, 37
murder, 20, 27, 85, 139–140
myths, about addiction, 2–24

N
narcotic, 13, 24, 30, 38
Narcotics Anonymous (NA), 22,
        80, 143, 148, 149, 151, 157
normality, 5

    lack of, 122–123
    return to, 142, 144

O
obsession, 37, 38, 39, 40, 42,
        71–72, 79–80
overcompensation, 120–121
overdose
    death from, 28, 29, 30, 33
    potential, 15
overreaction, 128–129

P
pain
    emotional, 37, 38, 52, 91, 94,
        96, 105, 120, 132, 141, 151
    physical, 5, 6, 23
painkiller, 23–24, 30
paranoia, 27, 38
parentified child, 91
parents
    addiction of, 2, 9–10, 43–45,
        59–61, 91, 95
        effects on children,
            112–135
        living with, 160–169
    conflict between, 2, 68, 99,
        104, 106–107, 119, 129
peacemaker, family, 91, 99–100
personality, addicted, 51–61
peyote, 22, 34, 42
phencyclidine (PCP), 22, 33, 42
pill
    as drug vehicle, 27, 28, 29, 30,
        32, 33, 34
    sleeping, 23–24, 29
placator, family, 91, 102–103
poison, 6, 15
polyaddiction, 36, 40

powder, as drug vehicle, 27, 28, 30, 33, 34
projection, 51, 52–53, 141
    moving to experiencing, 141–142
psilocybin, 35
psychedelics, 22, 24
psychosomatic illness, 91, 103–104

Q
quitting school, 7–8

R
rape, 139–140
reality
    denial of, 67
    losing touch with, 27, 34, 35
rebel, family, 91, 94–95, 108
recovery process, 141–153
relapse, 82–83
relationship
    family, 12, 22, 62–83
    intimate, 22, 78, 127–128, 152
    leaving, 63, 73, 74–75
responsibility
    excessive, 69–70, 115
    for recovery, 18
rigidity, 11, 17, 22, 51, 57–58, 133, 141
    moving to growth, 142–144
roles, family, 45, 91–108

S
scapegoat, family, 91, 93
scars, emotional, 3, 67, 90, 135, 137
sedative, 29

self-blame, 10–11, 73, 78, 112, 115, 116, 118, 134
self-esteem, 37, 63, 120
self-help group, 22, 156, 157–158
self-image, 22
self-pity, 167
self, standing up for, 72–73, 114
skin-popping, 34
smoking, as drug vehicle, 28, 32, 33
snorting, as drug vehicle, 27, 28, 33, 87
social drinking, 12
social services, 134, 137, 138
speed, 1, 6–7, 27, 39, 55, 73, 95, 130, 143
statistics, drug-related, 20, 50
stealing, 14, 21, 64, 95
stimulants, 26–29, 31, 36
stress, 47, 62, 102–107, 148
stroke, 15
substances
    addictive, 26–36
    mood-altering, 3, 6, 12, 13, 17, 24, 26, 56, 62, 79, 158, 168–169
suicide, 11, 20, 50, 88, 126
suppressor chemical, 4
switchboard, family, 91, 100–101
symptoms
    addiction, 46
    drug use, 27, 28, 29, 30, 31, 32, 33, 34
synesthesia, 33

T
THC, 5

therapist, 14, 20
  family, 46, 140, 157
THIQ, 4, 12, 15, 47
tolerance, 3, 5, 24, 47, 49
traffic accidents, 20, 23
tranquilizer, 29–30, 41, 152
treatment
  chemical dependency, 9,
    12–13, 14, 20, 78, 82, 147,
    149, 154–157
  for coaddict, 83
  for family, 78

U
upper cycle, 39–40
upper-downer cycle, 40–41

V
violence, 27, 28, 31, 45, 139, 167

W
warrior, family, 91, 107–108
whiskey, 1, 3, 16, 24, 31, 71
willpower, 12, 17, 24, 46, 158
wine, 13, 16, 24, 31
withdrawal, 9, 21, 29, 30, 31, 73